The Authors

TIM BAYLY and his wife Mary Lee have five children and twenty-some grandchildren. Tim is the author of *Daddy Tried: Overcoming the Failures of Fatherhood*. He has his BA from the University of Wisconsin–Madison and his MDiv from Gordon-Conwell Theological Seminary. Since 1996, Tim has served as senior pastor of Clearnote Church, Bloomington.

JOSEPH BAYLY and his wife Heidi have five children. After planting Clearnote Church in Indianapolis, Indiana, Joseph and Heidi moved to Cincinnati, Ohio, where they are working to plant Christ Church. Joseph has his BA from Vanderbilt University and his BDiv from Clearnote Pastors College.

JÜRGEN VON HAGEN and his wife Ilse have four children. Jürgen recently completed six years as vice rector of the University of Bonn, where he continues as professor of economics. A research fellow of London's Centre for Economic Policy Research, Jürgen is a member of the Academic Advisory Council of the Federal Minister of Economics and Technology in Germany and vice chair of the Portuguese Fiscal Council. He has been a consultant to the International Monetary Fund, the World Bank, the Federal Reserve Board, the European Commission, the European Central Bank, and the governments of several sovereign nations. Jürgen is senior pastor of Free Evangelical Church in Mülheim an der Ruhr, Germany.

THE

GRACE

OF

SHAME

THE GRACE OF SHAME

**7 Ways the Church Has Failed
to Love Homosexuals**

Tim Bayly
Joseph Bayly
Jürgen von Hagen

WARHORN
MEDIA

The Grace of Shame: 7 Ways the Church Has Failed to Love Homosexuals

Warhorn Media
2401 S Endwright Rd.
Bloomington, IN 47403
WarhornMedia.com

Cover design by Ben Crum
Interior layout by Alex McNeilly. Typeset in 11/14 pt. Adobe Garamond Pro.

Printed in the United States of America
21   20   19   18   17   1   2   3   4   5

ISBN-13: 978-1-940017-16-7 (paperback)
ISBN-13: 978-1-940017-17-4 (EPUB)
ISBN-13: 978-1-940017-18-1 (Kindle)

To all the
pastors, elders, and deacons
who are not ashamed
of Jesus' words

I have friends that are gay, and we study the Bible together.

Prince

If someone is gay and he searches for the Lord and has good will, who am I to judge? We shouldn't marginalize people for this. They must be integrated into society.

Pope Francis

Heterosexuality does not get you to heaven, so how in the world could homosexuality send you to hell?

Tim Keller

They have healed the brokenness of My people superficially,
Saying, "Peace, peace,"
But there is no peace.

Jeremiah 6:14

CONTENTS

FIRST, WE THANK OUR WIVES, MARY LEE BAYLY, HEIDI Bayly, and Ilse von Hagen. Mary Lee's faith in this project in particular brought this book through some very difficult moments. From the first, she was the one who most believed it was needed. Then, at critical junctures, when we were ready to give up, she kept saying, "You have to finish this book and get it out there. People need it."

> Houses and wealth are an inheritance from fathers,
> But a prudent wife is from the LORD.[1]

We thank Him for the beautiful gift He gave to each one of us.

Second, we thank the elders and pastors of Clearnote Church, Bloomington, and Clearnote Fellowship. These brothers have not flinched in their support of this tough word to the church today. The contemplation of the book's reception has pained them as much as it has us, but they have been steady in their affirmation of the necessity of the book for the salvation of sinners and the protection of the church.

---

1. Proverbs 19:14.

Our gratitude to God for His provision of these men and their wives and children is deep.

Third, there are many others who have given their time to this work, and without any payment: our reader David Canfield, our more-than-copyeditor and typesetter Alex McNeilly, our designer Ben Crum, our conceptual editors and podcast producers Nathan Alberson and Jake Mentzel,[2] and our wise counselor Tina Jacobson.

Finally, we thank our brothers and sisters in Christ who have led and joined us in living lives of repentance for sexual sin—particularly those who have repented of the sexual sins of sodomy and lesbianism. May God bless and keep you in His grace.

---

2. The podcast based on this book is called *The World We Made*.

THE

GRACE

OF

SHAME

Retain the standard of sound words which you have heard from me, in the faith and love which are in Christ Jesus.

2 Timothy 1:13

Words Matter

FIRST, A BRIEF WORD ABOUT WORDS SO YOU'LL UNDER-
stand the way this book uses them.

Historic Christian faith is committed to being nothing new. Orthodox Christians are orthodox because they are committed to remaining
old—two thousand years old, to be exact—in their faith and doctrine.
They hold to the plain teaching of Scripture.

God commands the shepherds of His flock to flee the new and novel, clinging to the old and revealed. Pastors and elders are God's conser-
vation officers, called to guard every truth the Holy Spirit has inspired
in every word of Scripture. Verse after verse hammers home this truth:

> And Jesus came up and spoke to them, saying, "All authority has
> been given to Me in heaven and on earth. Go therefore and make
> disciples of all the nations, baptizing them in the name of the Father
> and the Son and the Holy Spirit, teaching them to observe all that
> I commanded you; and lo, I am with you always, even to the end
> of the age."[1]

---

1. Matthew 28:18–20.

Guard, through the Holy Spirit who dwells in us, the treasure which has been entrusted to you.[2]

For the overseer must be above reproach . . . , holding fast the faithful word which is in accordance with the teaching, so that he will be able both to exhort in sound doctrine and to refute those who contradict.[3]

Many pastors today have decided the best way to conserve God's truth is to dispense with the words God uses in Scripture. They think confessing the truths of Scripture in the words of Scripture doesn't work anymore.

The authors of this book repudiate these tactics. For two thousand years orthodox Christians have confessed that it's not just the underlying truths of Scripture that are inspired by God, but the very words Scripture uses to declare those truths. Yes, those words were written by men, but every one of them is inspired by God. God Himself testifies, "all Scripture is inspired by God,"[4] so it is impossible to separate God's truths from God's words in Scripture.

We are all tempted to leave behind the words of Scripture that condemn our generation's pet sins. Today, sexual sins such as effeminacy, sodomy, and lesbianism are very popular, so even pastors in conservative churches are working to show how sensitive and understanding they are of these sins and those who commit them. One of the principle ways they demonstrate this sensitivity is by avoiding the very words God uses to condemn these sins.

We would never say so, but our abandonment of God's words condemning these sins shows that we think God was wrong to shame these sinners. That God shouldn't have been so hard on them in His language and His judgments recorded in the Bible.

Our generation is precious with our language and there are few places we've changed our language more than the way we speak of sexual sin. We kill God's truth by avoiding God's words, then we justify our

---

2. 2 Timothy 1:14.
3. Titus 1:7–9.
4. 2 Timothy 3:16.

shame at God's words by appealing to the pain of "sexual minorities."
We think gays and bisexuals are victims and shouldn't have the suffering
of minority status compounded by judgmental, self-righteous Christians who use insensitive language. Which is to say, biblical language.

But consider the infinite wisdom of God!

Before the world began, God knew what our own time would be like
and He inspired the words of His Word for us. The problem isn't God
or His words.

The problem is us.

Lacking faith, we repudiate God's Word in order to avoid what we
think of as "unnecessary offense." None of our changes in wording seem
like a big deal at the time, but as we leave each word behind, we cast
ourselves further adrift from our divine anchor which is the Word of
God that is eternally true. Instead of depending upon the power of the
Holy Spirit, we depend upon ourselves, forgetting what Jesus said:

> For truly I say to you, until heaven and earth pass away, not the
> smallest letter or stroke shall pass from the Law until all is accomplished.[5]

This book is our plea for the church to return to the words and truths
of Scripture in her loving witness to the effeminate, sodomites, women
who lie with other women, and similar "abominations."[6] If Christian
preaching is to be blessed with the power of the Holy Spirit, it must be
preaching that wields faithfully "the Sword of the Spirit, which is the
word of God."[7]

If we do this work, if we return to the words and truths of Scripture, we'll begin to really ask the question, Who loves sinners? Does the
church? Does it really love them? Does it love them enough to name
their sin and call them to repentance?

What about the effeminate, gays, lesbians, bisexuals, and transsexuals? Does the church love these men and women enough to name their
sin and call them to repentance?

---

5. Matthew 5:18.
6. Leviticus 18:22; Deuteronomy 22:5.
7. Ephesians 6:17.

That mention of "repentance" doesn't go down well with us. The world has hammered it into our heads that calling gays to repentance is hate speech.

You're just talking about gays' and lesbians' need to repent because you don't like them. You want to think you're better than they are. Haven't we gotten past this Us vs. Them thing yet? What about your own sin? Aren't you a sinner too? Why don't you try calling yourself to repentance?

Every gay man is not an alley cat, you know. Some of them are in lifelong loving and monogamous relationships. Some are even celibate! You think this is what Jesus would do? He loved sinners, and hung with the downtrodden and disenfranchised, didn't He? You think he wants us to go around telling gays and lesbians to repent or they'll burn in hell? Seriously?

Jesus came to save sinners, and He called them to repent out of His love for them.

If we follow Jesus today, we will also love sinners and call them to repent.

When He spoke to the woman at the well, our Savior gave us an example of how to love sinners. After asking her for a drink, Jesus didn't feign ignorance of her sin. Instead, He said to her, "Go, call your husband and come here."

The Samaritan woman responded, "I have no husband," but Jesus kept at it:

"You have correctly said, 'I have no husband'; for you have had five husbands, and the one whom you now have is not your husband; this you have said truly."[8]

Jesus saw the Samaritan woman's wound and brought it out in the open so she could be healed. Thus when she believed in Jesus, this was the testimony she took back to all the men of her village: "Come, see a man who told me all the things that I have done."[9]

None of the men listening to her were confused about what she meant by "all the things that I have done." They knew what she had done, so when they went with her to listen to Jesus they went to hear a man who would expose their sins. They went to hear a man who would

8. John 4:16–18.
9. John 4:29.

prove His love for sinners by showing them their sin and calling them to repentance and faith.

With the effeminate, gays, lesbians, bisexuals, and transsexuals, the church today must have the faith to follow Jesus' example.

Today, every Christian is being called to choose between the wide path of acceptance by the world and the narrow path of calling sexual sinners to repentance. Certainly we'll be misunderstood, scorned, and persecuted, but this is how Jesus suffered before us. No generation of Christians has ever escaped taking up their cross in following Jesus. He bore the cross first, so shouldn't we bear it with Him?

This refusal to speak God's words to sinners, using His language He has given us in His Word, is itself sin. When we are ashamed of God's words, we betray our duty. If we have any compassion for the effeminate, gays, lesbians, bisexuals, and transsexuals, we must return to speaking biblically about their sin and temptations. Pastors and elders particularly must not rob them of repentance by refusing to use the words God uses about their sin.

Some time back, one of our most admired pastors in North America was speaking at his denominational seminary to the men preparing to be pastors. When a student asked if he preached on homosexuality, he responded:

> I think the time is probably coming in which we're going to have to be more public in how we talk about homosexuality. And I haven't—I'm actually thinking quite a lot about it, as to how I will go about it, or how we should go about it, but I'm not prepared to give you, like, three bullet points yet. . . .
>
> . . . For me to do teaching in the worship service—"I am now going to give you the biblical teaching on homosexuality"—that has been a hard thing to do when my audience is so diverse.[10]

What does the diversity of our audience have to do with calling gays

---

10. Tim Keller and Bryan Chapell, "Question & Answer Session," *Ministry Lunches*, Covenant Theological Seminary lecture series, no. 5, mp3 audio, 2009, 29:07–30:03, https://www.covenantseminary.edu/resources/wp-content/uploads/sites/5/2014/11/Lecture-MinistryLunch-DrTimKellerDrBryanChapell-2009-QuestionandAnswerSession.mp3.

and lesbians to repent? What if our audience weren't diverse at all, but homogeneous? What if they were all homosexuals—then would he find it easier to teach on homosexuality?

Of course not.

The diversity in our churches has nothing to do with the reason we don't preach against effeminacy and homosexuality. The reason for our silence is really quite pedestrian. We are ashamed of Scripture's call to the effeminate and gays to repent. The true explanation is our own loveless hearts.

How can the authors say this?

Because we know ourselves. In our heart of hearts, we know as pastors that we would rather preach in a way that demonstrates to our congregations how sensitive we are to the LGBTQ alliance.

We don't want people to think we are condemning them. We don't want to be seen as oppressors of sexual minorities.

Calling actual sinners to repentance is sure to get us dissed and un-friended on Facebook. Our churches will get written up as a cult and people will avoid us like the plague. Even inside the church, church members will explain to us (as if we've never heard it) that preaching against homosexuality is sure to contribute to gays' feelings of insecurity, their propensity to substance abuse and depression, and their high rate of suicide.[11]

We know the routine. Naming the gay identity and gay sex as "abominations" must stop if we're going to keep high schoolers from committing suicide. It must stop if we're going to further the cause of meaningful dialogue and full equality for every color of the rainbow. It must stop if we want our churches to grow. It must stop if we want to stay in our pulpits.

Let's not fool ourselves. We don't call people to repent because we don't want to alienate our visitors. We don't want people to think we're homophobic. We don't want to lose members.

---

11. "The most exhaustive collation of published and unpublished international studies on the association of suicide attempts and sexual orientation with different methodologies has produced a very consistent picture: nearly all studies found increased incidences of self-reported suicide attempts among sexual minorities." Martin Plöderl et al., "Suicide Risk and Sexual Orientation," 723, as quoted in Lawrence S. Mayer and Paul R. McHugh, "Sexuality and Gender: Findings from the Biological, Psychological, and Social Sciences," The New Atlantis, no. 50 (Fall 2016): 68.

In a book on the ways the church has failed to love homosexuals, this is the only failure that really matters. This is the primary failure to be overcome. We will never help people until we're ready to really love them and call them to repentance.

To do that, we must be willing to lose our lives. We must be willing to take up our cross.

At the grocery store a couple nights ago, I[12] was scanning my purchases and the computer kept calling for help. It wouldn't allow me to continue until the woman overseeing the scanners came, put in her code, and hit some buttons. When she did, all was well for the moment, but when I continued scanning, it happened again. The woman came back, did her thing again, and left, but then it happened again. Finally, her supervisor came and looked at the screen.

"Oh, you have a recall," she said.

I was dense and asked, "What does 'recall' mean?"

"All the Dole bagged lettuce is recalled," she responded.

At this point she reached into my cart and pulled out another bag of Dole lettuce. Then she picked up the three bags I'd already scanned and off she walked with all my Dole lettuce.

But I needed salad, so leaving my purchased food in the cart next to the greeter, I went back to the produce section to get some other lettuce. There I stared at fifteen or twenty feet of wall display of lettuce I'd just taken my lettuce from a few minutes before. It was empty! There wasn't a bag of Dole lettuce left in that Meijer.

When I got home, I read the news and learned that people were sick and one person had died from eating Dole lettuce contaminated by *Listeria*. I had a couple bags of Dole lettuce in the refrigerator and I threw them out.

Sexuality is a lot more serious than lettuce contaminated by *Listeria*. Yes, sex causes people to die from crimes of passion and disease. Sex leads to pregnancy and about a quarter of our nation's pregnancies end with the murder of the unborn child. The sexual abuse of children causes boys and girls to suffer terrible emotional pain, often for the rest of their lives.

---

12. Throughout the book, all first-person stories and references are from Tim Bayly.

But what about our souls? How serious is it to stand before the judgment seat of God, and what place will sexual sin have on that dreadful day?

Listen to this warning from Scripture and notice the repeated references to sensuality and sexual sin, including specifically the sexual depravity of the Sodomites:

> But false prophets also arose among the people, just as there will also be false teachers among you, who will secretly introduce destructive heresies, even denying the Master who bought them, bringing swift destruction upon themselves. Many will follow their sensuality, and because of them the way of the truth will be maligned; and in their greed they will exploit you with false words; their judgment from long ago is not idle, and their destruction is not asleep.
>
> For if God did not spare angels when they sinned, but cast them into hell and committed them to pits of darkness, reserved for judgment; and did not spare the ancient world, but preserved Noah, a preacher of righteousness, with seven others, when He brought a flood upon the world of the ungodly; and if He condemned the cities of Sodom and Gomorrah to destruction by reducing them to ashes, having made them an example to those who would live ungodly lives thereafter; and if He rescued righteous Lot, oppressed by the sensual conduct of unprincipled men (for by what he saw and heard that righteous man, while living among them, felt his righteous soul tormented day after day by their lawless deeds), then the Lord knows how to rescue the godly from temptation, and to keep the unrighteous under punishment for the day of judgment, and especially those who indulge the flesh in its corrupt desires and despise authority. . . .
>
> These are springs without water and mists driven by a storm, for whom the black darkness has been reserved. For speaking out arrogant words of vanity they entice by fleshly desires, by sensuality, those who barely escape from the ones who live in error, promising them freedom while they themselves are slaves of corruption; for by what a man is overcome, by this he is enslaved. For if, after they have escaped the defilements of the world by the knowledge of the Lord

and Savior Jesus Christ, they are again entangled in
overcome, the last state has become worse for them
For it would be better for them not to have known t/
teousness, than having known it, to turn away from the nory —
mandment handed on to them. It has happened to them according
to the true proverb, "a dog returns to its own vomit," and, "A sow,
after washing, returns to wallowing in the mire."[13]

This lengthy part of 2 Peter is a helpful warning for us as we begin to
examine the church's errors concerning effeminacy and homosexuality
today.

We're not safe just because we're buying our lettuce with the brand
name Dole stamped on bags neatly arranged on shelves in our local
bright, clean Meijer store. Despite the brand name of the lettuce and
the cleanliness of the store, we must be on guard.

It's the same with the church and her leaders. We cannot simply
accept what pastors and Bible scholars say. We have to examine their
teaching, taking it to Scripture to see if they're giving us the truth or
twisting the truth to conform to the pattern of this evil world. Biblical
teaching and preaching will never provide comfort or a good hiding
place for sin—even (or especially) very popular sins.

The souls of the church of Berea were more noble than the souls of
the church of Thessalonica because "they received the word with great
eagerness, examining the Scriptures daily to see whether these things
were so."[14] When I was young, every church had a Bible study or Sunday
school class called "The Bereans," but in our soft and complacent day,
we don't like the spiritual gift of discernment.

It's so much easier to trust brand names and trademarks.

Yes, it's easier, but don't do it! In fact, don't do it with us and this
book. You don't know whether or not you can trust us, so examine our
words in the perfect light of God's words. See if we're faithful to use His
Word well.

It would be nice not to have to exercise discernment. It would be nice

---

13. 2 Peter 2:1–10; 17–22.
14. Acts 17:11.

only to have to draw a line between Islam and Christianity; between liberal and conservative Christianity; or, if we really must, between Roman Catholic and Protestant; and never ever between one conservative Christian who is Protestant and another conservative Christian who is Protestant.

But large doors hang on small hinges screwed into the door jamb with even smaller screws, and this doesn't make the hinges or screws unimportant. Sure, those screws are few and small, but without them things large and heavy come crashing down.

So now, let's move on to examine very carefully the teaching of some of the most valuable brand names of conservative Christianity in America today. Specifically, we will be examining what they have to say about the sins of effeminacy and homosexual intercourse.

As we do this work, we heed this warning from the Spirit of God:

Let not many of you become teachers, my brethren, knowing that as such we will incur a stricter judgment. For we all stumble in many ways. If anyone does not stumble in what he says, he is a perfect man, able to bridle the whole body as well.[15]

---

15. James 3:1–2.

Before they lay down, the men of the city, the men of Sodom, surrounded the house, both young and old, all the people from every quarter; and they called to Lot and said to him, "Where are the men who came to you tonight? Bring them out to us that we may have relations with them."

Genesis 19:4–5

CHAPTER 1

Some Personal History

CITIES ARE KNOWN BY THEIR SINS. LAS VEGAS IS "SIN CITY," but it isn't known for sodomy. San Francisco is known for sodomy, and so is our city of Bloomington, Indiana.

Recently a man who worked under the supervision of a Christian in our congregation went on Facebook and threatened to murder this Christian man. It's no shocker that he linked his obscene and murderous threats to the Christian's opposition to homosexuality. In Bloomington, this is our context for ministry.

So if you're wondering what our credentials are for writing a book about the failure of the church to love homosexuals, we answer that for the past twenty-five years our families have lived in a gay mecca. In His grace, God has placed us in a city where loving and calling gays and lesbians to repentance and faith in Jesus Christ has been a defining characteristic of our congregation's Gospel witness.

Bloomington is the home of Indiana University, and thus the home of at least one institution that has been at the forefront of the homosexualism[1] that defines our culture today. That institution is the Kinsey Institute.

---

1. In this book, the terms "homosexualism" and "homosexualist" refer to the movement to normalize sodomy, and that movement's advocates.

The institute is named for Alfred Kinsey, a professor of zoology who studied human sexuality and issued the Kinsey Reports in two volumes—the first in 1948 on male sexuality and the second in 1953 on female sexuality. Kinsey documented every form of sexual perversion and he stopped at nothing. Men he studied provided him with information on their molestation of little children down to two months of age. These men had raped little children and they were Kinsey's research.

Kinsey and his reports put Indiana University on the map. Today the Kinsey Institute is at the center of IU's campus and remains a source of pride to the academic community.

When I first took a call to serve as a pastor here in Bloomington, an older woman in the congregation asked to meet with me and we started what became a tradition that lasted for over a decade. Each week this mother-in-Israel (I'll call her Christiana) came over to the church and we sat and talked together. Christiana was a godly woman. She was also very smart. She'd grown up in Boston and attended Boston's Latin School, the best public high school in the country. Christiana went on to get her undergrad degree at Radcliffe, and was then awarded a graduate fellowship in astronomy at Harvard. There she met her future husband who, after completing his doctorate at Harvard (also in astronomy), applied for a position at Indiana University. Christiana accompanied him on his trip to Bloomington for the interview.

At the time, prospective faculty members and their spouses were expected to meet with Professor Kinsey so he could take their sexual histories. Thus it happened that Christiana sat down with Alfred Kinsey and answered all his prying and shameful questions.

Christiana mentioned this to me one day and I was incredulous. Earlier, Christiana had told me how Kinsey and his wife would invite faculty couples over to their house for dinner. After dinner, the Kinseys and their guests would move into the living room and Alfred would put some classical symphony on the record player and turn out the lights. There, in silence and darkness, the dinner party would commune with the music. Christiana said she and her husband went once and thought it so weird they never went back.

Yet now, this godly woman in her eighties was telling me Kinsey had taken her sexual history.

"What did you say?" I asked her.

Christiana let out a soft chuckle, saying "Well, I'm afraid he found me quite boring."

How many of us could say the same?

It made me nauseous to think of that destroyer of all that is virtuous worming his way into the most intimate life of my dear mother in the faith. The image of her having to submit to this wicked man's shameful inquiries in order to help her husband get a job was a defining moment in my life. Right then I came to understand that I, my wife, my sons and daughters, and all our Christian brothers and sisters in our congregation dwelt in Sodom.

As mentioned above, Kinsey published his first report on male sexuality back in 1948. It was a worldwide sensation. Everyone read about it and took its findings as justification for their own sexual perversions. *Everyone else is doing it, so what's the big deal?*

Maybe the wisest observation on Kinsey's report was made by the world-renowned anthropologist, Margaret Mead:

> In every society sex patterns depend on a careful and meticulous balance between ignorance and knowledge, sophistication and naïveté. . . . The Kinsey Report, by the publicity that has been given to this series of facts about extramarital and abnormal and unusual forms of sex satisfaction, has upset the balance in our society between ignorance and knowledge, between the things we don't mention, and the things we do. And it may be expected to have considerable effect in our society for that reason. Quite a good deal of our virtue has depended upon people not knowing what other people were doing—if they had known, they would have gone and done likewise; and when they weren't quite sure, sometimes they didn't.
>
> . . . Dr. Kinsey has limited himself to the description of a noninterpersonal and meaningless act. There is no suggestion of emotional content, of spiritual significance, of nonspiritual significance, of ethical significance. . . . He is perpetuating, to an extreme degree, the tendency to confuse sex with excretion—excremental rather than sacramental. . . . The major abstraction which I think any anthropologist from Mars would get out of the Kinsey Report . . . is

that (sex) is an impersonal, meaningless act which men have to per-
form fairly often—but oftener if they haven't been to school much.

. . . In the past, it was said, "It is better to marry than to burn."
Now we translate [the verse], "It is better to have an outlet of some
sort, because you've got to have an outlet of some sort." . . . So it's
just a question of which outlet and [Kinsey] suggests no way of
choosing between a woman and a sheep.[2]

A central plank in Kinsey's project was the destruction of the heterosexuality God created. Thus Kinsey composed a list of seven categories
of human sexuality, placing some component of homosexuality in six of
the seven. Meanwhile, Kinsey encouraged his colleagues to express their
sexual desires and he himself led the way, freely bedding whomever he
wished—both male and female.

They say the thief thinks everyone steals. Kinsey came to see his own
sexual degradation as normative. With all Scientism's authority mar-
shaled behind him, he declared his continuum of homosexual desires
to be scientific fact.

Almost seventy years later, it's no surprise Bloomington ranks as one
of the gayest cities in North America. Recently, the national gay pub-
lication *The Advocate* ranked Bloomington fourth among the "Gayest
Cities of America," adding this explanation:

This forward-thinking college town is a magnet city for gays in the
Grain Belt. It's also home to Indiana University, where Miss Gay
IU—said to be the first student-sponsored drag competition held
on any campus—is in its 20th year. The Kinsey Institute for Research in Sex, Gender, and Reproduction is also here, inspiring the
entire town to be heteroflexible.

Heteroflexible. Now it's clear why caring for gays and lesbians has
always made up a significant aspect of the pastoral work of our pastors,

2. Margaret Mead, "An Anthropologist Looks at the Kinsey Report," *Child and Family* 18, no.
4 (1979): 294–303. Mead's speech was given at a conference sponsored by the American Social Hy-
giene Association. The conference was held in New York City in 1948, two months after Kinsey's
first report was published.

elders, and Titus 2 women.[3] We never stop working with the effeminate, gays, and lesbians. Some are single, some married, and some get married. They love us and we love them. We hug and kiss them—remembering the New Testament's frequent command, "greet one another with a holy kiss."[4] We are in their homes and at their tables, just as they are in ours, eating with us and our children.

Those who repent and believe, we baptize and welcome to the Lord's Supper. Those who are unrepentant, we bar from the sacraments until they repent and believe. Those who go back to the pit God dug them from, we plead with them to return to Jesus. We ask lesbians who live together to repent and move apart. We ask single men who show no interest in the opposite sex if they struggle with their sexual identity. If an opera singer is using Craigslist to hook up while he's out on the road gigging, we ask him to come home. And the next time he goes out, if the sin gets the upper hand with him again, we send someone to go bring him home. If necessary, we ask him to break his contract.

Sadly, after countless hours of prayer and loving counsel; after our pastors and elders have pleaded with them to return to the Shepherd of their souls; some we excommunicate. And if they show up at their trial and cry as the judgment is pronounced and prayers are made, it wouldn't be the first time.

We do the same with the incestuous, the child abuser, the murderer, the thief, the deceiver, the fornicator, and the adulterer. Such were some of us.

We are committed to being an equal-opportunity church in our preaching, discipline, fellowship, and love. When it comes to diversity, pluralism, and inclusivity, Apple, Angie's List, and Indiana University have nothing on us. In fact, we have a leg up on them because, unlike them, we embrace Christians who say "no" to effeminacy, sodomy, lesbianism, and transsexuality.

We aren't writing this to brag about our ministries. We simply want

---

3. Titus 2:3–5: "Older women likewise are to be reverent in their behavior, not malicious gossips nor enslaved to much wine, teaching what is good, so that they may encourage the young women to love their husbands, to love their children, to be sensible, pure, workers at home, kind, being subject to their own husbands, so that the word of God will not be dishonored."

4. Romans 16:16; 1 Corinthians 16:20; 2 Corinthians 13:12; 1 Thessalonians 5:26; 1 Peter 5:14.

you to allow us to speak to you about what it really means to not be ashamed of Jesus and His words in our evil day.

My experiences with these sins don't start here in Bloomington. Back in 1974, I was living in San Diego and used a roommate matching service that quite inexplicably placed me in the home of a homosexual prostitute. He worked in his home, escorting his clients past me as I read in the living room. Since I was very poor back then, it took me a week or two to extricate myself from the horrors.

Then, in 1976, Mary Lee and I were married and moved to Madison, Wisconsin, where two of our closest friends were gay. A couple years later we moved to Boulder, then to the north shore of Boston. Across the decades, we have worked with gays and lesbians who have repented of their sins alongside adulterers, gossips, murderers, fornicators, and the proud.

When Mary Lee and I moved to Bloomington back in 1992, it was the height of the AIDS epidemic. Soon after we arrived, a mother in the church asked me to go up to Indianapolis to visit her son who was in a hospice dying of AIDS. She said she hoped I wouldn't mention his condition to anyone in the church.

Later, one of the older women of the church asked me privately what she should say to a friend of hers whose wife had just left him for her lesbian lover. This older woman had worked with the man's wife when they'd lived in Bloomington, and she thought they had been close friends. But now her friend was gone, her friend's husband was inconsolable, and this older woman and her husband had no idea what to say or how to help.

Then, another son of the congregation who made his living in opera also died of AIDS. After a memorial service out in New York City, the young man's body arrived in Bloomington and I was asked to officiate at the small committal service for family only. It was terribly sad. I'd never met the man and barely knew his parents, but there I was at the graveside, laying him to rest with these words:

> Man, that is born of a woman, hath but a short time to live, and is full of misery. He cometh up, and is cut down, like a flower; he fleeth as it were a shadow, and never continueth in one stay.

In the midst of life we are in death: of whom may we seek for succour, but of thee, O Lord, who for our sins art justly displeased?[5]

As you read this book, you may be tempted to think that we the authors have no compassion for sinners—particularly gays and lesbians. Yet it is precisely because of our compassion that we write. We have the faith to publish this book because we have seen the work of the Holy Spirit in bringing the effeminate, sodomites, and lesbians to repentance and faith in Jesus Christ. This book is not just our testimony, but even more the testimony of our congregations to the power of God's truth in calling and leading souls from death to life. All of us have faith that God is the God of truth, and that His truth brings us freedom from the terrible bondage of every sin.

We must take up our crosses and follow our Lord Jesus, trusting His Spirit to continue to lead men and women out of terrible bondage to forgiveness and freedom under the cross of Jesus.

---

5. "The Order for the Burial of the Dead," *The Book of Common Prayer* (1789 US edition), http://justus.anglican.org/resources/bcp/1789/Burial_1789.htm.

For they sow the wind and they reap the whirlwind.

Hosea 8:7

CHAPTER 2

The Church Yesterday

MY WIFE MARY LEE AND I GREW UP IN GODLY HOMES, but in high school we decided we were going to turn our backs on what we thought of as "traditional sex roles." Both of us saw male authority as old and in the way, so we became feminists.

Skip forward a few years after we were married. Since we were rebels against God's Creation Order, every decision in our home was a matter of negotiation, which meant we fought a lot.

One day, an older Christian man who knew us well, and loved us, took me aside to give me this simple admonishment: "Tim, God wants you to be the head of your home."

His rebuke went deep into my heart and I began to study what Scripture says about authority. It was the mid-seventies and I realized I lived in a culture that hated authority. Seeing how opposed to authority I was also, I knew it would be a very painful thing to begin to repent of this sin and lead in my marriage. Still, God gave me the grace to start down the path of repentance, and as time passed Mary Lee began to open up to my leadership.

Skip forward another few years. I'd graduated from seminary and Mary Lee and I were serving two churches of a yoked parish in Wisconsin's dairy land. Sadly though, we had chosen to minister in a denomination that required its churches and pastors to deny Adam's federal headship. For years they had been requiring each of their churches to have an equal number of male and female elders and they also required every search committee to sign an equal-opportunity form promising they were giving equal consideration to men and women for their pastoral vacancy.

Yes, I went into this sinful state of affairs with my eyes open. I told myself I could compromise on the matter because it was not a Gospel issue.

I also told myself what was important was the home—not the church. As long as husbands remained the head of their wives and fathers the head of their families, it would be okay for me to work alongside women elders and pastors.

When I was ordained, more than half the elders in our town church were women. In fact, the denomination also pressured churches to ordain very young elders, so one of the elders of the town church was a girl who had been ordained and began serving on the session when she was sixteen years old.

So there I was, living and serving in a terribly compromised position requiring me to deny the plain truth of Scripture that God forbade women to teach and exercise authority over men:

> But I do not allow a woman to teach or exercise authority over a man, but to remain quiet. For it was Adam who was first created, and then Eve. And it was not Adam who was deceived, but the woman being deceived, fell into transgression.[1]

Yet I told myself that, as long as I wasn't forced to give up the authority of husbands and fathers, I could live with women pastors and elders.

Because I'm writing this, you know that God had mercy on me and led me to repentance. He did it through the faithful witness of a woman elder and her husband, Evelyn and Don Jerred. With love and gentleness, together they led me to see the hypocrisy of my compromise, and in time Evelyn resigned from the eldership.

---

1. 1 Timothy 2:12–14.

Then Don finally agreed to serve as an elder and God used this godly couple to lead not only their young pastor, but the whole church to repent of our submission to the feminist juggernaut corrupting our denomination. In a few years our congregation no longer had any women willing to serve as elders. A few years after that we left the mainline Presbyterian Church (USA) for a biblical denomination that submitted to Scripture.

When I was being examined for transfer into our new denomination, I was asked what I believed about women officers. I responded that I had formerly supported them, but now I said, "I repent."

Yet many more pressure points appeared as the years went by, and it grieves me to admit that I have continued to find ways to be ashamed and hide from persecution for my biblical witness to God's beautiful gift of sexuality.

You think I'm the exception to the rule?

I'm afraid not. Rather, it's my observation that I am typical of conservative pastors, elders, deacons, and seminary professors.

Why all this about feminism? The battle lines are formed around homosexuality today, but the battles over sexuality have been going on long enough for the church to have established a track record in its response to the sexual revolution.

The first test of the church wasn't homosexuality, but feminism. The feminist rebellion gave us a chance to bear witness to the Fatherhood of God in man as male, but we chose to be silent.

Next our witness was tested concerning fornication. The children of our churches fornicated with one another, but we refused to bear witness against their fornication. We gave our own kids a pass on that sin.

Next our witness was tested by the sin of adultery. But instead of condemning and disciplining it in our churches, we cultivated a taste for it, learning to suck it up in our entertainment—just like the worldlings we lived among.

Next our witness was tested by divorce, which God says He "hates."[2] Our own sons and daughters and the members of our church families divorced one another and we refused to condemn or discipline them. Instead, we went along with society's "no-fault" divorce revolution, and

---

2. Malachi 2:16.

our pastors agreed to remarry anyone and everyone, without batting an eye.

What did we expect would happen when homosexuality reared its ugly head?

Anyone who examines the history will see that our past failures to be faithful witnesses in each of these other areas of sexuality is predictive of our present failures concerning homosexuality. All these failures are of a fabric.

What has been the quality of our witness to God's gift of sexuality these past few decades?

Let's go to the sin of feminism.

Some of us have signed on to egalitarian marriage. We deny that the husband is the head of the wife as Christ is the head of the church. We deny that the word "head" has any connotation of authority. We say the husband's authority is simply tie-breaking authority—not responsibility and leadership.

Outside marriage and the home, we say the senior pastor needs to be a man, but not the elders—they may be women. We defy Scripture's command that women not teach or exercise authority over men. We put women in our pulpits preaching and in our church classrooms teaching men. They teach in our seminaries and serve communion and lead our worship and teach our Sunday schools. If we're conservative, we excuse our actions by saying those women preaching and teaching are doing so under the authority of our board of elders, so it's really the elders who are exercising authority over men through these women.

Outside the Christian home and church, we say there's nothing wrong with women serving as policepersons, guards in a men's prison, lawyers, doctors, senators, judges, combatants in the armed forces, governors, prime ministers, and presidents. We tell the world male leadership is just a private Christian thing, assuring ourselves it's just the private lives of Christians God is concerned about.

We can imagine arguments are welling up in readers right now who want to disagree with this or that specific—if not the whole general idea that God has formed Adam and Eve with separate natures and purposes. We don't have time to discuss where and how we should witness to God's Creation Order of Adam then Eve among unbelievers.

It's complicated and that discussion would subvert the immediate task at hand.

What we must acknowledge, though, is that for decades we've been trimming the application of this Creation Order everywhere we can, because we want to avoid taking up our cross. We don't want to be called "sexists." We don't want to be called "fundamentalists." We don't want to appear patronizing or selfish. We don't want to look like Neanderthals. We don't want our wives or daughters to sneer at us. We don't want to be shamed on Facebook. We don't want to be hauled up before our city's civil rights commission or our company's human resources department. We don't want to be frozen out of the conversation at the family reunion.

We don't want to suffer the world's hatred.

But hindsight shows that our failure to witness to God's decree of male responsibility and authority hasn't placated the worldlings even one little bit. The faithless compromises have only emboldened the wicked to turn their attack to the even more fundamental bifurcation of man into male and female. So now we live in a world demanding the replacement of God's male and female with endless gender identities reinforced by changes in our words and phrases.

We no longer speak of "sex" as the foundation of our personhood given us by God when He made us male or female. Instead, we speak about "gender" which has no reference to body parts. The body parts of male and female are now dismissed by the politics of identity. The calling given us by God at the moment of conception known as "sex" has been replaced by the choice each individual makes of this or that "gender identity."

Young men and women are pressured to listen to whatever sinful desires they find within themselves and stake out any identity along the gender continuum that strikes their fancy at the moment. And no, they needn't worry about their mind changing in a couple months or years. Gender is plastic, so if the gender identity they first settle on doesn't suit them long-term, they can change it and there's no harm done. There are as many genders as points on a compass, so choice reigns supreme.

The sexual rebellion has spread across our world and it didn't begin with sodomy. Every violation of God's Creation Order matters—

whether that violation is women ruling and exercising authority over men, or women lying with women and men lying with men.

The homosexuality opposing God's heterosexuality is the natural fruit of the abandonment of man's responsibility and authority that has been pervasive in our congregations and denominations for decades now. It was inevitable that the repudiation of manhood and womanhood in the relationship between sex and authority would bear the fruit of repudiation of manhood and womanhood in sexual identity—then in sexual intimacy. If men and women have no God-ordained pattern of fitting together in authority and submission, why submit to the God-ordained pattern of fitting together in our identity or body parts? If one of these aspects of God's Creation Order is a private Christian truth, why object to our culture abandoning these other aspects of God's sexual order?

Maybe woman's rebellion against man doesn't seem like such a terrible thing, but here's what God says about rebellion:

> For rebellion is as the sin of divination,
> And insubordination is as iniquity and idolatry.[3]

Rebellion is a contagious disease. Pull on one thread and another unravels.

We have refused to teach God's Creation Order in making Adam first, then Eve, so now we are surrounded by neighbors who also reject God's Creation Order of Adam and Eve in favor of Adam and Steve. We have refused to confess our manhood and womanhood outside the home and the church as a bright shining light in a very dark day. We have refused to teach our children to confess their manhood and womanhood. We have failed to call them to be our culture's salt and light through their male or female sexuality.

Behind it all, we have removed fruitfulness from our marriage beds. We have followed the worldlings in their pursuit of children as a lifestyle choice rather than the obedience of faith in God's command to every married couple to "be fruitful and multiply."[4]

---

3. 1 Samuel 15:23.
4. Genesis 1:22, 28; 8:17; 9:1, 7; 35:11. See also Malachi 2:15.

Yes, Scripture condemns homosexuality. Yet there's even more in Scripture that condemns male abdication, female rebellion, adultery, divorce, fornication—and the list goes on.

Sadly, where we still find some opposition to sodomy among Christians, we suspect it's mostly due to sodomy's yuck factor—what the Apostle Paul refers to as the homosexual's "unnatural" intercourse. We are squeamish about this sin in a way we are not squeamish about other sexual sins. We think of ourselves as honoring God and Scripture in opposing homosexuality, but we might do well to stop and examine our true thoughts and motives. How much do we really care about gays and lesbians?

Again, the present homosexualist crisis has not come out of nowhere. It has a context which indicts the church for our past witness.

As many reading this will know, in 2015, we in the United States watched our Supreme Court rule that homosexual marriage is a basic human right protected by our Constitution. We watched Indiana throw in the towel on their effort to protect the First Amendment rights of citizens to witness against sins Scripture declares to be an abomination before the Lord, and we watched states across our nation pass legislation criminalizing counseling that helps homosexuals to repent of their sin and embrace the manhood or womanhood given them by God.

The rest of this book will document how we *then* watched as church officers responded to this growing rebellion by repenting of their former "insensitivity" and declaring they now believe in homosexual orientation, by promoting the phrase "godliness is not heterosexuality," by welcoming into their congregations those who continue to identify as "gay Christians," and by joining the crusade to criminalize counseling that helps men and women to love and live the sex God made them.

In other words, church leaders are running for cover. We'll detail how in the rest of this book. And yet, as we move forward, let's remember that our Lord promised His church that the gates of hell would never prevail against her.[5] There is plenty of time to right our course, but we must understand how and why we have left God's straight and

---

5. Matthew 16:18.

narrow path. The rest of this book is an effort to show how we veered off course, and what we should do about it.

Will we be faithful to those caught in the bondage of every form of sexual sin, from fornication to effeminacy to adultery to incest to bestiality to masturbation to women lying with women and men with men?

May God give us faith to clear away the rubble and begin to testify once more that from the beginning He made us male and female. This time without shame.

Do not be deceived; neither fornicators, nor idolaters, nor adulterers, nor effeminate, nor homosexuals, nor thieves, nor the covetous, nor drunkards, nor revilers, nor swindlers, will inherit the kingdom of God.

1 Corinthians 6:9–10

CHAPTER 3

ERROR 1

Removing the Sin of Effeminacy (Part 1)

AFTER THE DEATH OF ROCK STAR DAVID BOWIE, *SLATE* ran a piece titled "Was David Bowie Gay?" At various times Bowie said he was gay, then straight, then bisexual—each according to his mood at the time.

The writer of the piece is gay. You feel him suppressing his anger at Bowie for not simply coming out as a gay man. Near the end of his piece, he gives this brilliant summary of the state of gayness today:

> I believe that cultural gayness is something that can and does exist *apart from* homosexuality. Gays may have developed the set of cultural practices that define gayness, or what some call the "gay sensibility" or "gay aesthetics," but they need not be its only practitioners. Indeed, straight people (or whatever Bowie might have been) are theoretically just as capable of doing cultural gayness as gays are—and indeed, some may do it better.[1]

---

1. J. Bryan Lowder, "Was David Bowie Gay?" *Slate*, January 11, 2016, http://www.slate.com /blogs/outward/2016/01/11/was_david_bowie_dead_at_69_gay_the_glam_rocker_had_a _complicated_relationship.html.

Gay sensibilities, gay aesthetics, gay speech, dress, and manner-isms—all this gayness exists independent of homosexual intercourse. As the author says, a gay or effeminate identity may or may not be combined with gay sex.

Scripture condemns both. The gay, soft, or effeminate identity and gay sexual intercourse both deny the sex God made us.

Whether or not David Bowie committed sodomy, God made David Bowie a man and it was his duty to live in submission to his manhood. God called him to live manly, but Bowie rebelled and spent his life living gay. Effeminate.

The Apostle Paul lived in a time as sexually decadent as our own and he knew Bowie well. Writing to the believers in Corinth—the San Francisco of the Roman Empire—Paul warned them that *arsenokoitai* (literally, "men who lie with males") will not inherit the kingdom of God. Immediately before that warning, Paul declared that *malakoi* (literally, "soft men") will not inherit the kingdom of God:

> Do you not know that the unrighteous will not inherit the kingdom of God? Do not be deceived; neither fornicators, nor idolaters, nor adulterers, nor effeminate [*malakoi*], nor homosexuals [*arsenokoitai*], nor thieves, nor the covetous, nor drunkards, nor revilers, nor swindlers, will inherit the kingdom of God.[2]

The Apostle Paul refers to *malakoi* and *arsenokoitai* as two distinct categories of sinners:

1. men like David Bowie who are effeminate; and
2. men who lie with males (those who commit homosexual acts).

Men who betray their manhood by playing the woman[3] will not be in Heaven.

---

2. 1 Corinthians 6:9–10 (NASB).

3. "The word *malakoi* [referred] to adult males who . . . actively feminized their appearance and manner as a means to attracting [male] partners." Robert A. J. Gagnon, "A Comprehensive

Immediately we hear the sputtering and ridicule:

Are you serious? "Soft" men? You have to be kidding me! God judges men by how soft or hard they are? So Christian men have to be macho? The guy that bench presses 300 pounds gets into Heaven but the guy who can't do pushups is out of luck?

Our sexually debauched world mocks, yet the Word of God abides forever.

Until recently, the church translated the Greek word *malakoi* using the English word "effeminate." And it's in the middle of a sin list which comprises "the unrighteous" who will not "inherit the kingdom of God."

Note this list of sinners is preceded by the warning "Do not be deceived." The warning is addressed to the believers in the Corinthian church, so the Apostle Paul is warning the Corinthians that men will attempt to deceive them concerning the sins of fornication, idolatry, adultery, sodomy, thievery, covetousness, drunkenness, reviling, swindling, and effeminacy. What is the deception Paul warns against?

The false teacher's deception is the denial that these sins will bar a man from Heaven. He flatters sinners concerning the state of their soul and their hope of eternal life—thus the apostle's warning, which he gives twice, once at the beginning and once at the end of this sin list.

Faithfulness to God's Word requires us to repeat this warning in our churches today.

Are evangelical churches doing so?

No. The sin of effeminacy is never mentioned in our churches today. In fact, our modern Bible translations have removed "effeminacy" from this sin list in 1 Corinthians 6.

The Apostle Paul warned that neither "soft men, nor men who lie with a male" will inherit the kingdom of God, but the translators of our new Bible versions compressed the two categories of sinners into one: "men who practice homosexuality."

Having removed "effeminate," they justified their deletion of this word with footnotes such as this:

and Critical Review Essay of *Homosexuality, Science, and the 'Plain Sense' of Scripture*, Part 2," 229, accessed January 22, 2016, http://www.robgagnon.net/articles/homoBalchHBTReview2.pdf.

The two Greek terms translated by this phrase refer to the passive and active partners in consensual homosexual acts.[4]

Past generations of English Bible readers were able to read the word God's Holy Spirit inspired. Their Bibles always translated the Greek word *malakoi* into English, so everyone knew effeminacy was a sin distinct from homosexual intercourse, and that both sins excluded men from the kingdom of God.

Here's a record of this faithfulness on the part of Bible translators which continued unbroken until the past few years:

Wycliffe Bible (1395): "neither lechers against kind, neither they that do lechery with men"

Tyndale Bible (1536): "nether weaklinges nether abusars of them selves with the mankynde"

Luther's Bible (1545): "noch die Weichlinge noch die Knaben-schänder"

Geneva Bible (1599): "nor wantons, nor buggerers"

King James Version (1611): "nor effeminate, nor abusers of them-selves with mankind"

Douay-Rheims Bible (1899): "nor the effeminate, nor liers with mankind"

J. B. Phillips New Testament (1961): "neither the effeminate, the pervert"

The New Jerusalem Bible (1985): "the self-indulgent, sodomites"

---

4. 1 Corinthians 6:9, English Standard Version. The Christian Standard Bible does the same, translating the words *malakoi* and *arsenokoitai* as "males who have sex with males" and adding this footnote: "Both passive and active participants in homosexual acts."

New American Standard Bible (1995): "nor effeminate, nor homosexuals"

Every Bible listed above was faithful to bring into the receptor language the distinction the Apostle Paul made between men who are soft, self-indulgent, or effeminate; and men who bed other men. Six centuries of Roman Catholic and Protestant Bibles were faithful to translate both *malakoi* and *arsenokoitai*.

But then, as homosexualists began to pressure the church to accept effeminacy, homosexual lust, and homosexual practice the past couple of decades, our modern Bible translators removed *malakoi* from their translations.

Their justifications for this removal are inexcusable. Past Bible scholars all left the word intact and translated it correctly, so they had many faithful witnesses across the centuries that they could have easily followed. Furthermore, even if they declined to learn from past Bible translators, they could have learned the meaning and proper translation of the word by studying the many centuries of usage provided in the literature of the ancient world. Unlike the next word in the Apostle Paul's sin list, *arsenokoitai*, the usage and meaning of *malakoi* is thoroughly documented in ancient literature.

For example, in *Histories*, Herodotus makes the observation that "soft men [*malakoi*] are wont to spring from soft countries."[5]

In a speech from *The History of the Peloponnesian War*, Thucydides records a warning given to an assemblyman who might precipitously vote for war for fear of being "thought a coward [*malakos*] if he did not."[6]

Twice in the *Athenian Constitution*, Aristotle speaks of the *malakoi*: once when it is recorded that men of the house of Codrus were no longer chosen as king "because they were thought to be luxurious and to have become soft [*malakous*]"; and again when it is said that "some of the kings proved cowardly [*malakous*] in warfare."[7]

---

5. Herodotus, *Histories* 9.122.
6. Thucydides, *The History of the Peloponnesian War* 6.18.
7. Aristotle, *Athenian Constitution*, fragments, Ἐκ τῶν Ἡρακλείδου περὶ Πολιτειῶν; ibid., ch. 3.

Closer to the time of the New Testament, Josephus writes:

After this, the Israelites grew effeminate [*malakōs*] as to fighting any more against their enemies, but applied themselves to the cultivation of the land, which producing them great plenty and riches, they neglected the regular disposition of their settlement, and indulged themselves in luxury and pleasures.[8]

Again, Josephus:

Do not you pretend to be either more tender [*malakōterous*] than a woman, or more compassionate than a mother; but if you be so scrupulous, and do abominate this my sacrifice, as I have eaten the one half, let the rest be reserved for me also.[9]

A century after the New Testament, Diogenes Laertius writes:

It is said that when he laid it down as Zeno's opinion that a man's character could be known from his looks, certain witty young men brought before him a rake with hands horny from toil in the country and requested him to state what the man's character was. Cleanthes was perplexed and ordered the man to go away; but when, as he was making off, he sneezed, "I have it," cried Cleanthes, "he is effeminate [*malakos*]."[10]

In their later usage of *malakos* and its cognates, the early church fathers again demonstrate there is no basis for today's Bible translators telling the church the *malakoi* are merely passive partners in homosexual intercourse.

Clement of Alexandria writes:

We are not to laugh perpetually, for that is going beyond bounds; nor in the presence of elderly persons, or others worthy of respect,

---

8. *Antiquities* 5.2.7.
9. *Wars of the Jews* 6.3.4.
10. *Lives of Eminent Philosophers* 7.5.

unless they indulge in pleasantry for our amusement. Nor are we to laugh before all and sundry, nor in every place, nor to everyone, nor about everything. For to children and women especially laughter is the cause of slipping into scandal. And even to appear stern serves to keep those about us at their distance. For gravity can ward off the approaches of licentiousness by a mere look. All senseless people, to speak in a word, wine "Commands both to laugh luxuriously and to dance," changing effeminate manners to softness [*malakian*]. We must consider, too, how consequently freedom of speech leads impropriety on to filthy speaking."[11]

And:

To such an extent, then, has luxury advanced, that not only are the female sex deranged about this frivolous pursuit, but men also are infected with the disease. For not being free of the love of finery, they are not in health; but inclining to voluptuousness, they become effeminate [*malthakōteron*], cutting their hair in an ungentleman-like and meretricious way, clothed in fine and transparent garments, chewing mastich, smelling of perfume.[12]

We could multiply such citations, but the point has been made: the effeminate or soft men sin not only when they play the woman in bed, but also when they play the woman in the way they live outside the bedroom. Playing the woman is not something the *malakoi* take on and off before and after intercourse. It is their lifestyle. It is their character, and this sinful character is condemned by both the ancient world and God in His Word. It is the sin of effeminacy. The Bible declares the effeminate will not enter Heaven.

Living contrary to the sex God made him bars the effeminate man from the kingdom of God.

Note carefully that not all the sins in this sin list are sins committed on a bed. Some argue today that *malakoi* must refer exclusively to the passive partner in homosexual intercourse because it appears in the

---

11. *The Instructor* 2.5.
12. Ibid. 2.18.

list between two other forms of sinful sexual intercourse—adultery and men-who-lie-with-a-male.

There's no question effeminacy in intercourse is also condemned here. Robert Gagnon writes:

> Since [*malakoi*] is sandwiched in between the terms *pornoi* . . . and *moichoi* (adulterers) on the one side and *arsenokoitai* (men who lie with a male) on the other side, it is probable that *malakoi* too has to do with immoral sexual relations.[13]

Still, effeminacy doesn't start when the effeminate man gets in bed with another man—just as adultery doesn't start when the adulterer gets in bed with a woman other than his wife. Both sins begin much earlier, and so Jesus warned against lustful looks saying they are the adultery of "the heart."[14]

Does an adulterous heart bar one from the kingdom of God, or is it only adulterous intercourse that is warned against here? To ask the question is to answer it. Man looks at the outward appearance, but God looks at the heart.[15]

Also, consider that, immediately prior to the adultery/effeminacy/men-who-lie-with-a-male list of three, we have the fornication/idolatry/adultery list of three. Fornication and adultery are sinful forms of sexual intercourse, but idolatry is far more than sexual sin. Thus the proximity of sins of sexual intercourse is no argument for the claim that effeminacy is only that sin committed by the passive partner when a man lies with another man.

Even if we were to claim each of the first five sins in this sin list are sexual sins, this is no reason to limit the sinfulness of effeminacy to its commission during sexual relations. Effeminacy is the denial of one's manhood decreed by God, and thus effeminacy is a sexual sin even when it is committed by a man who is all alone. Fornication of the heart and fornication of the body, adultery of the heart and adultery

---

13. "Dale Martin and the Myth of Total Textual Indeterminacy," accessed December 11, 2016, http://www.robgagnon.net/DaleMartinResponse.htm.

14. Matthew 5:27–28.

15. 1 Samuel 16:7.

of the body, effeminacy of the heart and effeminacy of the body. In 1 Corinthians 6:9–10, the Apostle Paul is not simply condemning sins of the bedroom, but also sins outside the bedroom. Sins of the heart.[16]

There's another reason the church has never taught that *malakoi* only refers to homosexual intercourse. Why would the Apostle Paul warn passive partners in homosexual intercourse they will not inherit the kingdom of God and then immediately give the same warning to *all* participants in homosexual intercourse? Both the active and passive partners in homosexual intercourse are "men-who-lie-with-a-male," so the two warnings would be redundant.

But when we restore the full meaning of *malakoi* to the text, we return to the historic church's doctrine that what is being condemned is not merely playing the woman during the sexual act, but playing the woman in life itself. Neither the effeminate nor men-who-lie-with-a-male will inherit the kingdom of God.

If the Apostle Paul had warned "neither temptresses nor adulterers will inherit the kingdom of God," it's hard to imagine today's Bible translators reassuring the church that the word "temptresses" was just referring to the passive partner in extramarital intercourse and had nothing to do with the temptress lifestyle described in Proverbs 7:

> "I have spread my couch with coverings,
> With colored linens of Egypt.
> I have sprinkled my bed
> With myrrh, aloes and cinnamon.
> Come, let us drink our fill of love until morning;
> Let us delight ourselves with caresses."
>
> . . . .
>
> With her many persuasions she entices him;
> With her flattering lips she seduces him.[17]

Again, in this same text the Apostle Paul warns neither "thieves, nor

---

16. "Let it also be remembered that immorality, according to the Bible, does not consist exclusively in outward sins, but also in sins of the heart; as covetousness, malice, envy, pride, and such like." Charles Hodge, commentary on 1 Corinthians 6:9.

17. Proverbs 7:16–18, 21.

the covetous" will inherit the kingdom of God. Why not compress these two categories of sinners into one, following the example our modern Bible translators have set with *malakoi* and *arsenokoitai*?

As an experiment, let's leave out "the covetous," translating the warning "men who pursue dishonest gain" and adding this as a footnote:

> The two Greek terms translated "men who pursue dishonest gain" refer to the passive and active participants in theft.

Should we put out some new Bibles that scratch our ears here, too? We live in such a covetous age. Wouldn't it be a relief never again to have to read God's warning that "the covetous" will not inherit the kingdom of God? This would allow us to live a covetous life in which we could look and yearn and fantasize just as long as we didn't give in completely and touch.

You begin to see the can of worms Bible publishers and their translators have opened up by deleting the sin of effeminacy from Scripture.

What caused them to turn against their fathers in the faith of past centuries who were faithful to warn the effeminate? Was some ancient text discovered that brought new light to this word's meaning? Have modern Bible scholars discovered something Bible scholars of past centuries didn't know?

No, the citations from ancient sources listed above demonstrate that the meaning of *malakoi* has always been clear. It's not scholarship that made the changes, but the growing hostility of our culture toward Scripture's doctrine of sexuality—particularly its condemnation of sodomy and effeminacy.

The meaning of *malakoi* has come under assault from two directions.

First, the homosexualists began to argue *malakoi* had *nothing* to do with homosexual intercourse. Wanting to normalize same-sex intercourse, they began to claim *malakoi* meant "soft men" *only*. It didn't refer to men lying with men, but only to men lacking moral fiber and courage.

Conservatives responded that *malakoi* certainly does refer to men who engage in homosexual intercourse. There is no lower point to which the effeminate sinks than allowing another man to penetrate him; but working hard to hammer the point home, they left the main thrust of the meaning of effeminacy behind. In theological battle, we're often tempted to move so far from one error that we commit another one. Thus they defended the teaching of Scripture that homosexual intercourse is wrong, at the cost of denying *malakoi* had any meaning outside of homosexual intercourse.

Right here, it's important we recognize that no sin has ever been deleted from Scripture without sinful reasons. It wasn't just overzealousness on the part of conservatives that caused *malakoi* to be removed from Scripture. Another way of saying it is that there was nothing about winning the battle against homosexualists' denial that homosexual intercourse is sin that required anyone to delete God's condemnation of effeminacy. It wasn't the heat of the battle that caused *malakoi* to be left behind, but fear of the hoots and catcalls that greet anyone today who condemns "soft men" or "the effeminate," anyone who repeats the Bible's warning that soft men will not be in the kingdom of God. While showing ourselves faithful and courageous in denouncing the sin of homosexual intercourse, we can quietly leave behind the old-and-in-the-way sin of homosexual identity.

People trust us now that we've defended the Bible's condemnation of homosexual intercourse, so let's cut ourselves some slack and get rid of the sin of effeminacy. It's such an awkward sin to try to define. How on earth do you say what effeminacy is? Won't everyone think we're saying femininity itself is sinful? Won't it look like we're putting down women? How do I recognize an effeminate man and what am I supposed to say to him? What does repentance look like for an "effeminate"?

As Herodotus observed, soft men are wont to spring from soft lands, and from the days of *Blackhawk Down* to today, the entire world has known the United States of America is soft. Reflecting the character of the men and women of her nation, the American church is filled with soft men and hard women who have no fear of God as they delete words from His Word.

The two lies being told about the meaning of *malakoi* in 1 Corinthians 6:9 are mirror images of each other: on the one hand are liberals who claim *malakoi* doesn't refer to homosexual intercourse, but only to matters of character such as cowardice and the absence of firm moral principles; and on the other hand are conservatives who claim *malakoi* doesn't refer to matters of character such as cowardice and the absence of firm moral principles, but only to homosexual intercourse.[18]

I suppose we could summon within ourselves gratitude for conservatives standing against liberals' attempts to justify sodomy—if only we were able to remain ignorant of the way their departure from the consensus of past centuries contributes to the church turning a blind eye to the sin of the "gay Christian" identity movement. But we're not ignorant and the damage they're doing to sinners within and without the church is incalculable.

So which group should we call "liberals" and which "conservatives"? I guess the answer to the question would depend upon whether you are more appalled by men denying their manhood in private bedrooms or in public life.

18. The exception among conservative scholars is Robert Gagnon, who translates *malakoi* in 1 Corinthians 6:9, "effeminate males who play the sexual role of females." Gagnon writes, "the meaning of *malakoi* in 1 Cor 6:9 probably lies somewhere in between 'only prostituting passive homosexuals' and 'effeminate heterosexual and homosexual males.'" See Robert A. J. Gagnon, *The Bible and Homosexual Practice: Texts and Hermeneutics* (Nashville: Abingdon Press, 2001), 306–308.

Does not even nature itself teach you that if a man has long hair, it is a dishonor to him?

1 Corinthians 11:14

Removing the Sin of Effeminacy (Part 2)

MEN WHO ARE EFFEMINATE WILL NOT BE IN HEAVEN.
This is a stunning Gospel truth that is perfectly suited to call the soft
men of our androgynous age to repentance and faith. Those who are
being saved eat this warning and find it sweeter than honey.

Yet there are Christians who can't bear the shame of this warning
and find it bitter to their taste. Such men often hide behind requests
for clarification:

*What does it mean to be effeminate? Some men are more sensitive by
nature—it's how God made them. They like poetry. They'd rather go to an
opera than hunt or play a pickup game of hoops. Is it some kind of sin for a
guy to read poetry and wear pink shirts?*

Maybe readers are irritated at the equating of poetry, opera, and
pink with effeminacy, but these words aren't ours. They are the words
of Christians who deny that effeminacy is sin and mock any attempt to
define it.

After all, we live in a culture drowning in effeminacy, so the removal
of *malakoi* (as the last chapter showed has been done in modern Bible
translations) suits us just fine. Removing the word saves us from having

to define the sin of softness or effeminacy and having our definition met by hoots and hollers.

Yet while scholars ban the sin from inclusion in modern Bibles and from conversations in polite society, the sin is alive and well, and frequently spoken of in impolite society. Take, for instance, comedy clubs and locker rooms: there men can talk about effeminacy all they want, although they don't use the words "soft" or "effeminate."

They say "gay." The guy that gets out of fights by crying is "gay." The guy that wears lavender or drives a Prius is "gay." The guy that plucks his eyebrows is "gay." Soccer players who dive are "gay."

And when a comedian or jock says a guy is "gay," no one is so dense as to think it means the guy hooks up with men instead of women. He just means the guy is soft and effeminate. He calls him "gay" because the way he dresses, talks, and acts isn't manly.

In the time of the Apostle Paul, the Greek word *malakos* was used in this same way. Everyone understood the word didn't merely designate the passive participant in sodomitic relations. It meant the guy was soft and effeminate. Today they'd say the guy is "gay," "soft," or a "wuss." And if they're in a men's locker room, they might call him an even more expressive term.

Historians describing the almost exclusively pederastic (man and boy) practice of sodomy in ancient Greece have for some time now been matter-of-fact about the distinction between men who are womanish and men who engage in sodomy. For instance, here is gay activist and classicist David Halperin, author of the constructivist classic *One Hundred Years of Homosexuality*:

> Being a womanish man is not the same thing as being a homosexual, and the sexual activities that typically identify someone as belonging to the first category are quite different from the sexual activities that identify someone as belonging to the second.[1]

So again, how is it that homosexualists are matter-of-fact in their

---

1. David M. Halperin, "Greek Love: An Exchange," *The New York Review of Books*, April 26, 1990, accessed January 4, 2017, http://www.nybooks.com/articles/1990/04/26/greek-love-an-exchange/.

discussions of the distinction between womanish men and sodomites while today's New Testament scholars delete this distinction from the Apostle Paul's first letter to the Corinthians?

Even fifteen centuries after the Apostle Paul said the *malakoi* would not inherit the kingdom of God, the meaning of *malakoi* was still so clear that John Calvin made this comment on the Apostle Paul's warning:

> By effeminate [*malakoi*] I understand those who, while they may not openly become prostitutes, nevertheless show how unchaste they are by the use of pandering words, by effeminate bearing and dress, and other means of attracting attention.[2]

Malakoi appears four times in the Greek New Testament—once here in 1 Corinthians 6:9 and three other times when Jesus was defending John the Baptist. John rebuked Rome's governor, Herod, for having his brother's wife, and Herod rewarded John's godliness by throwing him into prison and later cutting off his head.

While John was still alive in prison, he sent a few of his disciples to ask Jesus some questions. After Jesus answered them, He turned to the crowd that was listening to the exchange and said:

> What did you go out into the wilderness to see? A reed shaken by the wind? But what did you go out to see? A man dressed in soft clothing? Those who wear soft clothing are in kings' palaces![3]

Looking at the Greek words Jesus used, He said John the Baptist was not "a man dressed in *malakois*" ("soft garments"), and that "those who bear themselves soft [*malaka*] are in kings' palaces."

The Puritan pastor Matthew Henry summarized Jesus' statements about John:

> Was he a man clothed in soft raiment? If so, you would not have

---

2. *The First Epistle of Paul the Apostle to the Corinthians*, Calvin's New Testament Commentaries, trans. John W. Fraser, ed. David W. Torrance and Thomas F. Torrance (Grand Rapids: Eerdmans, 1960), 124.

3. Matthew 11:7–8.

gone into the wilderness to see him, but to the court. You went to see one that had his raiment of camel's hair, and a leathern girdle about his loins; his mien and habit showed that he was dead to all the pomps of the world and the pleasures of sense; his clothing agreed with the wilderness he lived in, and the doctrine he preached there, that of repentance.[4]

When Jesus pointed out that John the Baptist was not a man to wear soft clothing, nor to bear himself soft, Jesus used this same word *malakos* used by the Apostle Paul.

Jesus continued: "But what did you go out to see? A prophet? Yes, I tell you, and one who is more than a prophet."

Then Jesus ended his defense of John with a statement most of us find jolting: "From the days of John the Baptist until now the kingdom of heaven suffers violence, and violent men take it by force."[5]

Violent men taking the kingdom of heaven by force?

You see what Jesus is saying. John the Baptist wasn't one of the *malakoi*, because the *malakoi* aren't out in the wilderness.

Prophets don't dress themselves soft. They don't have an effeminate bearing. They don't dress and talk and carry themselves like women.

Prophets aren't gay.

John the Baptist was a man's man, and men who want to enter the kingdom of God will imitate him. Like John the Baptist, violent men will take the kingdom of heaven by force.

Here's Matthew Henry again:

This violence denotes a strength, and vigour, and earnestness of desire and endeavour. . . . They who would enter into the kingdom of heaven must strive to enter; that kingdom suffers a holy violence; self must be denied, the bent and bias, the frame and temper, of the mind must be altered; there are hard services to be done, and hard sufferings to be undergone, force to be put upon the corrupt nature;

4. Comments on Matthew 11:8, *Commentary on the Whole Bible*, http://www.ccel.org/study/Matthew_11.
5. Matthew 11:7–9, 12.

we must run, and wrestle, and fight, and be in an agony. . . . The violent take it by force.[6]

The violence Jesus makes reference to is not violence against other men, let alone women and children. It's violence against our own sinful lusts. It's violence in opposing our desire to be soft and vacillating in our pursuit of the kingdom of God.

Jesus isn't commending machismo. He's commending the manly pursuit of eternal life.

The final use of *malakos* in Scripture is in Luke's account of Jesus' defense of John the Baptist: "But what did you go out to see? A man dressed in soft clothing [*malakois*]? Those who are splendidly clothed and live in luxury are found in royal palaces!"[7]

Jesus' words about John the Baptist fill out the Apostle Paul's warning that *malakoi*, soft or effeminate men, will be barred from the kingdom of God.

What about our Lord Jesus? Was He soft or effeminate?

All the pictures of Jesus in our Bible storybooks make Him look gay. Locks of beautiful, blondish hair. Pretty smile. He's wearing a long flowing gown that's pressed and clean. His hand is extended in a "Come to Me" gesture.

It's all a lie. This Jesus is an idol. We have turned Jesus into the soft, effeminate man we are ourselves. So there in the Bible storybooks we read to our children is an image of the kind of man who adorns the cover of every cheap romance novel, the kind of man adored by a certain kind of woman.

Is this the portrayal of Jesus we read in the four gospels? Would the Jesus pictured in the Bible storybooks have responded this way to a compliment paid to His mother?:

One of the women in the crowd raised her voice and said to Him, "Blessed is the womb that bore You and the breasts at which You

---

6. Comments on Matthew 11:12.
7. Luke 7:25.

nursed." But He said, "On the contrary, blessed are those who hear the word of God and observe it."[8]

Would He have responded this way when His mother and brothers were asking Him to come out to talk to them?:

Someone said to Him, "Behold, Your mother and Your brothers are standing outside seeking to speak to You." But Jesus answered the one who was telling Him and said, "Who is My mother and who are My brothers?" And stretching out His hand toward His disciples, He said, "Behold My mother and My brothers! For whoever does the will of My Father who is in heaven, he is My brother and sister and mother."[9]

Would the Jesus of our Bible storybooks say this?:

If anyone comes to Me, and does not hate his own father and mother and wife and children and brothers and sisters, yes, and even his own life, he cannot be My disciple.[10]

But beyond the firmness of His character and demands, what does the Bible say about Jesus' physical appearance? Only one statement and it's not in the gospels, but Isaiah's prophecy:

He has no stately form or majesty
That we should look upon Him,
Nor appearance that we should be attracted to Him.
He was despised and forsaken of men,
A man of sorrows and acquainted with grief;
And like one from whom men hide their face
He was despised, and we did not esteem Him.[11]

---

8. Luke 11:27–28.
9. Matthew 12:47–50.
10. Luke 14:26.
11. Isaiah 53:2–3.

Jesus was not a mama's boy, nor was He a lady's man.

Jesus was a prophet and prophets aren't gay.

Jesus was a man of firm principles. He wasn't one of the *malakoi*. He wasn't soft, but hard, and it was His great love that made Him hard. Love for His Father. Love for sinners. Love for us.

Luke tells us Jesus "set his face to go to Jerusalem."[12] Jesus had a manly resolve to go there and die. He was firmly committed to doing the will of His Father.

Jesus' hardness was particularly evident in His zeal for His Father's honor. It was this zeal that led Jesus to go to the temple and whip the merchants, turning their tables upside down:

> And He entered the temple and began to drive out those who were buying and selling in the temple, and overturned the tables of the money changers and the seats of those who were selling doves; and He would not permit anyone to carry merchandise through the temple. And He began to teach and say to them, "Is it not written, 'My house shall be called a house of prayer for all the nations'? But you have made it a robbers' den." The chief priests and the scribes heard this, and began seeking how to destroy Him; for they were afraid of Him, for the whole crowd was astonished at His teaching.[13]

John the Baptist and Jesus were hard men—but not hard in the sense that they lacked compassion and were impossible to please. They were hard men in the sense of being self-denying, principled, and firm in their commitment to compassion, justice, mercy, truth, and the glory of God. They were hard in their pursuit of the kingdom of God. They sought it with a holy violence.

John the Baptist and Jesus didn't have a gender identity. They had their manhood and they never took it off. Or rather, they never stopped putting it on.

The Bible doesn't talk about gender identity. It doesn't speak of homosexuality and heterosexuality.

---

12. Luke 9:51 (KJV).
13. Mark 11:15–18.

The Bible talks about male and female, man and woman, and it warns us soft men will not enter the kingdom of God.

Soft is not what God made man to be. Look at man's sexual organ and consider the simple truth that godliness for man means living in obedience to his body. His body is hard in taking initiative and bearing responsibility, and this is the reason soft men will not enter the kingdom of God. They are in rebellion against God and who He made them to be.

By necessary implication, the opposite is true of woman. Hard women will not enter the kingdom of God.

Hard is not what God made woman to be. Look at woman's sexual organ and consider the simple truth that godliness for woman means living in obedience to her body. Her body is soft in receiving man's initiative and bearing the fruit of his initiative through her gift of life, and this is the reason hard women will not enter the kingdom of God. They are in rebellion against God and who He made them to be.

God created man and woman profoundly dichotomous, and the man or woman who seeks to blur His dichotomy will not enter the kingdom of God.

Jesus emphasized this fundamental dichotomy when He stated that "from the beginning, God made them male and female."[14] Thus we are to obey our sexual identity. Yes, in our sexual coupling; but no less so in the way we live our lives.

Sex is much more than intercourse. Sex is all of life. No matter where we go, we never stop being boy or girl, man or woman, and thus we never escape God's command for us to confess the manhood or womanhood He decreed for us at the moment of our conception.[15]

So now, does it matter whether a man is unmanly? Whether he plays the woman? Whether he is soft and effeminate? Does it matter whether

---

14. Mark 10:6.

15. Here the objection may be raised that some are born hermaphrodites, and the argument made that since not everyone is able to know what sex to confess, no one needs to confess their sex. This rhetorical ploy is a perfect example of what someone has spoken of as the "modern morbid habit of sacrificing the normal on the altar of the abnormal." Those born hermaphrodites suffer from their condition and should be the objects of our charity and understanding, yet we can't use their condition to justify our rebellion against the sex God plainly made us.

a woman is manly? Whether she plays the man? Whether she is hard and butch?

If so, we'd better do the hard work necessary to grow in our understanding of what it means for a man to be soft and a woman hard.

As men, we don't want God to bar us from His kingdom because we didn't understand effeminacy is sin and thus failed to live out the manhood He decreed for us.

Sure, it's easy to say these body parts do or don't go with those body parts. It's easy to condemn homosexual intercourse because the body parts don't fit together. But God designed sex to be much more than body parts. He made us to dress and speak—and even to pursue the kingdom of heaven—in a manly way.

Jesus' reference to men who dress effeminately should be read in the context of Deuteronomy 22:5:

> A woman shall not wear man's clothing, nor shall a man put on a woman's clothing; for whoever does these things is an abomination to the LORD your God.

Calvin comments:

> This decree also commends modesty in general, and in it God anticipates the danger, lest women should harden themselves into forgetfulness of modesty, or men should degenerate into effeminacy unworthy of their nature. Garments are not in themselves of so much importance; but as it is disgraceful for men to become effeminate, and also for women to affect manliness in their dress and gestures, propriety and modesty are prescribed, not only for decency's sake, but lest one kind of liberty should at length lead to something worse.[16]

"Something worse" is effeminacy. Calvin explains that men wearing the clothing of women and women wearing the clothing of men is

---

16. From Calvin's exposition of the Seventh Commandment in *Commentaries on the Last Four Books of Moses*, trans. Charles W. Bingham.

condemned by God because it leads to effeminate men and immodest women.

But that's not all it leads to, is it? Notice the order of the Apostle Paul's warnings: first, he warns against effeminacy, then he warns against men lying with men. Men wearing the clothing of women and being effeminate naturally leads to the next sin listed by the Apostle Paul: men lying with men.

Which is to say, the full-blown cult of homosexuality eviscerating the beautiful diversity of sexuality from our culture today is the natural fruit of the cult of effeminacy we have been drowning in for decades.

Who led us into effeminacy and androgyny?

There were many influences, but speaking personally, we don't think we can overemphasize the influence of music. There's a great deal of truth to the statement that a church's music tells you more about its doctrine than the preaching. So what does our music tell us about the character of our culture?

My first rock concert was Steppenwolf. A couple of us from the church youth group wanted to take in a concert, so we went into Chicago and took in a Steppenwolf concert.

At some point during the concert, I needed to use the bathroom and found one, deep in the bowels of the amphitheater. It was gross. Guys were passed out on the floor with their heads in the urinals. It should have been a clue to me, but I wasn't ready to see.

The musicians strutted their stuff:

> Why don't you tell your dreams to me
> Fantasy will set you free
> Close your eyes girl
> Look inside girl
> Let the sound take you away

It was my first rock concert and many others followed: Jethro Tull, New Riders of the Purple Sage, Chambers Brothers, Cheap Trick, Sly and the Family Stone, Alice Cooper, Dylan, Grateful Dead, Genesis, Pink Floyd, Yes, Albert Collins, Springsteen . . .

What all the concerts had in common was idolatry. Rock stars were gods and we worshiped them. And most of the musicians packaged themselves in androgyny.

They cultivated effeminacy. They wore tight jeans and made gestures in the direction of their private parts. They wore makeup and jewelry and scarves. Their shirts were unbuttoned to the navel or waist. They gyrated and pranced. And their hair—am I channeling the Apostle Paul, here?—their hair was colored, permed, and shamefully long.

> Does not even nature itself teach you that if a man has long hair, it is a dishonor to him?[17]

Still today, fifty years later, androgyny is one of musicians' favorite shticks. They preen in the mirror. They're pretty like a woman, but strong like a man. And right there between pretty and strong is their sex appeal—only now, women like Danica Patrick and Ronda Rousey are getting in on the act.

Rock concerts gave us stars halfway between man and woman and we loved it.

Mick Jagger once said in an interview, "rock and roll is sex." He's right. Rock and roll is also rebellion. Put sex and rebellion together and you have Mick Jagger's androgyny.

What about Christian musicians—are they different?

In past centuries the church got it. Think of Handel's *Messiah*. Handel took Scripture at face value and composed music that was biblical, celebrating the violence of God against His enemies:

> He that dwelleth in heaven shall laugh them to scorn;
> The Lord shall have them in derision.

Immediately following, Handel has a tenor sing:

> Thou shalt break them with a rod of iron;
> Thou shalt dash them in pieces, like a potter's vessel.

Handel simply wrote a musical setting for Psalm 2:4, followed by

---

17. 1 Corinthians 11:14.

Psalm 2:9. The themes of judgment and God's wrath are found through-out Psalms, which is the hymnbook of Christ's church. Yet when was the last time we sang such themes in our worship?

In past centuries, the church had no problem singing these themes in worship. Here's *Harvest Hymn* from colonial times:

> The fields are all white, the harvest is near,
> The reapers all with their sharp sickles appear.
> To reap down their wheat, and gather in barns,
> While wild plants of nature are left for to burn.
>
> Come then, O my soul, and think on that day,
> When all things in nature shall cease and decay.
> The trumpet shall sound, the angels appear,
> To reap down the earth, both the wheat and the tare.
>
> Come hither, ye tribes, your sentence receive,
> No longer my spirit shall strive and be grieved.
> My judgment is right, my sentence is just,
> Come hither, ye blest, but depart all ye cursed.
>
> O sinners, take thought, and seek ye the Lord,
> I have not been jesting, it is Christ's own word.
> That those who done good, in glory shall stand,
> While those who done evil shall surely be damned.

Imagine this hymn being one we looked forward to singing in church each year as Thanksgiving approaches. Why do we no longer sing in celebration of the judgment and wrath of God?

Our music tells us our doctrine. We sing soft songs because we're soft men who have soft doctrine. So how can we correct this?

Once we catch a vision for living out our manhood by faith as a command of God, then we begin to see that the real essence of man-hood isn't having a buff body. Rather, it's taking initiative and respon-sibility for others. It's saying no to our lusts and pleasures. It's having faith to do things that look like they are going to absolutely destroy any future of us getting jobs or having a church. It's calling others to follow you by faith on that same crazy path. It's taking weight on yourself, and carrying it for other people. In a word, it's fatherhood.

Much more needs to be said on this topic, but this is not the book for it.[18] As we bring this chapter to an end, let's close with a few statements to get us thinking about the distinction between men who are manly and men who are effeminate:

Hard men build civilizations; soft men destroy them.

Hard men build families; soft men destroy them.

Hard men preach; soft men wonder and suggest.

Hard men are zealous in worship; soft men are passive.

Hard men love discipline; soft men hate it.

Hard men love soft women; soft men love hard women.

Hard men raise sons and daughters; soft men raise persons.

Hard men are loud in worship; soft men are loud in whining.

Hard men are in the kingdom of God.

Soft men are not.

---

18. Please read Tim Bayly's *Daddy Tried* (Bloomington, IN: Warhorn Media, 2016) for more practical teaching on what growing in this area looks like. It is written to men who are fathers, future fathers, or hope that someday they might be ready to be fathers, by the grace of God.

When a woman falls in love with me, I feel guilty. I am convinced that it's pure obstinacy that keeps me from reciprocating her passion. As I explain to her that I'm gay, it sounds, even to me, like a silly excuse; I scarcely believe it myself.

Edmund White

There is no good tree which produces bad fruit, nor, on the other hand, a bad tree which produces good fruit. For each tree is known by its own fruit. For men do not gather figs from thorns, nor do they pick grapes from a briar bush. The good man out of the good treasure of his heart brings forth what is good; and the evil man out of the evil treasure brings forth what is evil; for his mouth speaks from that which fills his heart.

Luke 6:43–45

CHAPTER 5

ERROR 2

The "Gay Christian" Error

LIBERAL CHURCHES AND DENOMINATIONS WERE THE battlefield for the normalization of homosexuality thirty years ago, but that battle has been won.

Now the homosexualist forces have turned their attention to conservative Christian churches and denominations. These are the last hold-outs against the mainstreaming of homosexual practice and identity in our culture, and a key part of homosexualists' strategy for dealing with Bible-believing Christians is blurring the battle lines. Much of their blurring is done through deceptive slogans and labels. We'll spend the next six chapters examining several of them.

First, the label "gay Christian." Can someone live gay and be a Christian? The label "gay Christian" is intended to answer that question with a resounding *yes*, but the way this phrase is used is confusing.

Consider that if someone says, "I'm a gay Christian," there's no one who is going to respond, "No you're not!" It wouldn't be nice. If we heard someone responding by pointing out that "gay Christian" is an oxymoron, and that the Apostle Paul said, "such *were* some of you,"[1] we'd likely think to ourselves:

---

1. 1 Corinthians 6:11. Emphasis ours.

How would you know whether he's a Christian or not? Can you see into a man's heart? Do you know what he believes? All of us are saved by grace. What makes you think God hasn't saved him? You think being gay is some sort of unpardonable sin or something?

It's impossible to know what someone's saying when they claim the identity of "gay Christian," and that's precisely the point. People get timid and shut their mouths and minds around such a controverted issue where everyone's feelings are at fever pitch, so the label "gay Christian" is allowed to stand without refutation and has become perfectly respectable.

Also notice how the label "gay Christian" has changed through the years. Thirty years ago everyone knew precisely what it meant. "Gay Christian" indicated a full gay lifestyle—gay identity and gay sexual intercourse. Now, though, the "gay Christian" label is also being used to refer to only half a gay lifestyle—gay identity without gay sexual intercourse.

The problem for the "gay Christian" camp nowadays is how to make inroads with conservative Christians, the sorts of Christians who compare nature with Scripture and find the two agree. Christians may be squeamish about discussing reproductive organs, but generally they are humble enough to acknowledge how the man's and woman's genitalia witness to God's plan, not just for sexual intercourse, but for all of life. They see how the man's and woman's reproductive organs contain a certain hard and soft logic that is inescapable. Those with eyes to see the meaning our Creator has written into our body parts easily understand that man is made to initiate and woman to receive. Again, the book of nature and the Book of God agree.

The other problem for the "gay Christian" camp is that not everyone within the homosexualist camp is happy about this change in the meaning of "gay Christian."

Here's an explanation given by the homosexualist website, the Gay Christian Network, on their page titled "The Great Debate":

When it comes to gay Christians, there's one question that causes more debate than any other: Does God bless gay relationships? Or are gay Christians called to lifelong celibacy?

Further down the page, we find the names of the two sides:

Side A . . . believes that God blesses same-sex marriages.
Side B . . . believes that God calls gay Christians to lifelong celibacy.[2]

The Gay Christian Network is split between "Side A" and "Side B," with both sides claiming the phrase "gay Christian." All the gays and lesbians using this phrase are proud of their gay identity. What they differ over is gay intercourse and marriage. Gay Christians of Side A do it, and gay Christians of Side B don't.

Keep in mind that proponents of Side A have no illusion that they'll be accepted by conservative Christians any time soon. They are gay all the way through, and that's that. It is the proponents of Side B who hope for the acceptance of conservative Christians, so while sharing the gay identity of Side A, they promise not to share Side A's gay intercourse and marriage.

Now of course Side B gay Christians would want to change the way we said that. They would protest that the reason they don't have gay intercourse is not that they want the acceptance of conservative Christians, but that gay intercourse is wrong.

There's a hidden premise here: the gay Christian who says he isn't going to have gay intercourse is counting on Christians to give him a pass on his effeminacy and the direction of his sexual desires. His major premise is that having a gay identity and gay desires is not sin—that the Bible doesn't condemn his homosexual desires or identity. All that's required of gay men is that they avoid touching. And as we noted in our last chapter, modern Bibles remove Scripture's condemnation of "soft men," thus providing perfect cover for these gay Christians. In other words, the gay Christian must not lie with other gays, but he shouldn't suffer guilt for his homosexual lusts. He should feel free to be as "gay" and "effeminate" in his carriage and identity as he wants. There's nothing wrong with homosexual desires and being one of the *malakoi* as long as you don't actually touch another man. It's the same with the gay

2. Accessed August 19, 2017, https://www.gaychristian.net/the-great-debate/.

Christian woman: she can desire other women and be as hard or butch as she wants, so long as she doesn't actually touch another woman.

This is directly contrary to the teaching of Scripture.

As we saw in the chapter on effeminacy, God says none of the effeminate, the *malakoi*, the soft men (and, by extension, the hard women) will inherit the kingdom of God.

First, in Romans 1, the Apostle Paul warns against homosexual desires themselves:

> God gave them over to degrading passions; for their women exchanged the natural function for that which is unnatural, and in the same way also the men abandoned the natural function of the woman and burned in their desire toward one another.[3]

Men burning in their desire toward one another—what we liltingly refer to as "the desire for same-sex intimacy"—is not morally neutral. By itself it is evil. No touching needed. Scripture says, "God gave them over to degrading passions."

Note also that, in the order of the words in 1 Corinthians 6:9, God's condemnation of gay, soft, effeminate, womanly men comes before His condemnation of men lying with men. What happens when a man gives himself to effeminacy and playing the woman? Not being able to say no to his lusts, the effeminate decays until he finds himself in bed with another man. A man giving himself over to softness is well on the way to giving himself over to bedding another man.

Only a halfhearted love for gays and lesbians—or a complete lack of discernment—would allow us to go along with this halfway covenant.

Honestly. The man who has faith in the power of the Holy Spirit to change the heart of men is not conniving at the "gay Christian" lust or identity when someone he loves reveals it about himself. Rather, this man is faithful to push and pull this way and that, seeking the reason his brother in Christ wants to identity himself with this utter degradation. Maybe he can't figure it out right away, but the one thing he's absolutely sure of is that something is terribly wrong.

---

3. Romans 1:26–27.

If we start identifying everyone in church by their besetting lusts and sins, where will it will stop? Instead of introducing ourselves as Ben, Joe, and Sam, will we shake hands and say, "I'm Gay Gary," "Incest Isaiah," or "Pedophile Peter"? In the entryway after worship, will we introduce our friends to visitors as "Greedy Gus," "Thief Tim," and "Zoophile Zane"? If not, why not?

The answer is obvious: no one's trying to soften the church up for the removal of the shame of men who lust after children, boys who lust after their brother or sister, lazy men who live off other men's work, greedy men, or men whose sexual desire is for animals.

Then why would the church assist men who burn with desires for other men to make their desires public, thereby helping them remove their shame? We don't treat other sinners this way.

Does it honor God to go along with this label "gay Christian"? Is it right to privilege homosexual lusts and effeminacy over other sexual sins? Is this privileging helpful to our children as they come to adolescence and are deciding whether to obey God and confess the sex He made them? Is it even helpful to this man who is halfway down the path to bedding other men—this man who, although he'd deny it, seems to be precious with his desires and softness?

Now let's look at the fruit of this "gay Christian" movement.

Over the course of the past couple years, the highest profile proponent of the Side B "gay Christian" identity within the evangelical church here in the United States was Wheaton College's lesbian chaplain, Julie Rodgers. This past year Ms. Rodgers very publicly flipped from Side B to Side A. Listen to how she announced her change:

Because I care about the gaybies and it's right to keep it real even if it comes at a cost, it seems like a good time to share some of the ways my thinking on how to best love and support sexual minorities has evolved through the years. . . .

Though I've been slow to admit it to myself, I've quietly supported same-sex relationships for a while now. . . .

. . . I've become increasingly troubled by the unintended consequences of messages that insist all LGBT people commit to lifelong celibacy. No matter how graciously it's framed, that message tends to contribute to feelings of shame and alienation for gay Christians.[4]

A couple days after Rodgers's announcement, I was speaking with a man who has gained some prominence promoting the "gay Christian" strategy within the Presbyterian Church in America. He told me of a conversation he'd had with a Christian brother earlier that week. He said he'd told the other man how angry he was over Rodgers flipping sides.

Why?

Claiming to be a proponent of Side B is the way Rodgers had succeeded in getting hired by Wheaton College, the most visible evangelical institution in these United States. Yet now here was Ms. Rodgers leaving behind the whole celibacy thing, even going so far as to say she'd been opted out "for a while now." I think a large part of my friend's anger came out of his fear that the gains the homosexuals of Side B had brought to the gay community within the conservative Christian church would be jeopardized by Ms. Rodgers bringing back together the two sides of gay identity and gay sex.

Rodgers was the coming-out party for gay Christians in the evangelical world, yet less than a year after Wheaton hired her, she was telling everyone that, during the previous year—while she worked as a chaplain to Wheaton's gay Christian students—she had not really been opposed to gay sex. As she put it, "I've quietly supported same-sex relationships for a while now" (she means intercourse).

Note that Rodgers's statement makes a claim that is equally true for all gay Christians, whether Side A or Side B. She speaks of her fellow gay Christians as "sexual minorities," and this phrase is critical to understanding the "gay Christian" movement's growing infiltration of the Bible-believing church.

Every American has been hard-wired by the media and all the teachers and profs he's sat under to think of himself as a faithful advocate for minorities that others (who are less sensitive) discriminate against. Beat-

---

4. "An Update on the Gay Debate: evolving ideas, untidy stories, and hopes for the church," July 13, 2015, accessed March 5, 2016, https://julierodgers.wordpress.com/2015/07/13/an-update-on-the-gay-debate-evolving-ideas-untidy-stories-and-hopes-for-the-church/.

ing their chests over racism continues to be one of the principal subjects in the regional and national assemblies of southern Presbyterian and Baptist churches, so it's perfectly understandable that white southerners now condemning their fathers and grandfathers for not marching on Selma will want to get ahead of the ball on these freshly minted minorities. Fifty years from now they don't want their own grandchildren voting on overtures condemning them for their discrimination against sexual minorities.

With that in mind, meditate on Rodgers's phrase "sexual minorities." This is the perfect tune to play to set conservative Christians back on our haunches in the current climate of political correctness, and Rodgers knows it.

Wheaton got itself a lesbian chaplain to work with the "sexual minorities" on campus, and while she was on Wheaton's payroll she wasn't just an advocate for lesbians and gays, but also bisexuals and the transgendered.

To Rodgers, "all LGBT people" are "sexual minorities."

So this is the state of our evangelical union: the same year Bruce Jenner was "transitioning" and appeared on the cover of *Vanity Fair* with an airbrushed bosom clothed in a push-up bustier, Wheaton's lesbian chaplain served as his advocate by claiming the moral equivalence of sodomy, lesbianism, bisexualism, and transgenderism. Wheaton's gay Christian chaplain declared her solidarity with men like Jenner, saying that, along with "gaybies," transsexuals also suffer from the church's discrimination against "sexual minorities."

There is a silver lining to this dark cloud. When Rodgers manipulates her readers through the use of this language of political extortion, she opens up a truth we'll keep front and center throughout this book: the only way to recognize homosexualists' ploys is to remember that God's Word lumps all sexual sins together. Until we begin to substitute other sexual sinners for the gays and lesbians that homosexualists trot out as "sexual minorities," we'll not begin to see through their exceedingly sophisticated and deceptive rhetoric.

Hiring a young, pretty, and athletic gay Christian woman as a chaplain to serve the spiritual needs of your students who are "sexual minorities" is likely to get a much better reception from the trustees and alumni than hiring a fat middle-aged man who identifies as a "pedophile Christian." It may seem harsh to point this out, but such manipulations and lies go down smoothly and it takes a rude jolt to wake us up from our stupor.

What is our biblical basis for saying gays, lesbians, bisexuals, and transsexuals can continue in their lusts and live out their identity in Christ, but rapists and pedophiles cannot? That gays and transsexuals are victims of the church's discrimination against "sexual minorities," but adulterers and pedophiles are not? That gays and transsexuals are kind and gentle, but fathers who rape their daughters are monsters?

Take pedophilia as an example: this wicked sexual orientation would seem to be as deeply seated in the psyche as gayness or lesbianism. Look at the recidivism rate. Look at the statistics on the average number of children the pedophile has corrupted before he is caught. How can anyone argue that the pedophile's sexual orientation is any less deep-seated than the sexual orientation of the gay or lesbian?

So then, why aren't we as sympathetic to the pedophile as we are to the gay man or lesbian woman? No one can argue pedophiles are not sexual minorities, so on what basis do we deny them the affirmative action Julie Rodgers and her gay and lesbian compatriots receive from the administration and trustees of Wheaton College?

The "gay Christian" movement is contrary to God's Word whether or not the particular person claiming the label is sexually active. God doesn't create any man gay or any woman lesbian. Jesus told us that, from the beginning, God made them male and female.[5] God made man to love and desire woman—not another man. He made woman to love and desire man—not another woman. This is as true today of our sons and daughters as it was true of God's son and daughter, Adam and Eve. Thus it is that Scripture warns that soft men and sodomites will not inherit the kingdom of God. They are turned against who God made Adam to be—and every man since. The Word of God says these men have "abandoned the natural function of the woman and burned in their desire toward one another,"[6] and every Christian trembles to read

---

5. Matthew 19:4.
6. Romans 1:27.

this judgment, turning to plead with God to rescue these souls He has given over to degrading passions.

No matter how early the onset or deep-seated the temptations suffered by those who call themselves "gay Christians," we must not allow them to blame nature or nature's God. The Father Almighty creates only men and women, and each of those men and women choose whether they will confess the sex God made them as an act of faith and obedience. They may choose to rebel against God. They may deny their sex and tell the church they're "gay." They may add that they promise not to engage in gay sex. But they've already committed solidarity with the *malakoi*, the soft men who are their fellow "gaybies." They've already rebelled against God by giving themselves to gay lusts, gay mannerisms, gay dressing, gay talking, gay relating with other men and women . . .

Need I go on?

The Bible tells us if any man is in Christ, he is a new creation. Old things have passed away. Behold, all things are new.[7]

Note it's not *most* things, but *all* things.

If it's acceptance we want, the acceptance of conservative Christians and membership in Christ's church is the easiest (and hardest) thing in the world. All one must do is repent and believe in the shed blood of Jesus Christ. In other words, if the man identifying himself as a "gay Christian" were to drop the "gay" part and seek membership, no problem. It's the compression of "gay" and "Christian" that makes things difficult, because the gay identity, gay desires, and gay intercourse are rebellion against God.

---

7. 2 Corinthians 5:17; Revelation 21:5.

Heterosexuality does not get you to heaven, so how in the world could homosexuality send you to hell?

Tim Keller

The whole truth is generally the ally of virtue; a half-truth is always the ally of some vice.

G. K. Chesterton

For if the bugle produces an indistinct sound, who will prepare himself for battle?

1 Corinthians 14:8

CHAPTER 6

ERROR 3
The "Godliness Is Not Heterosexuality" Error

THE "GAY CHRISTIAN" STRATEGY IS GETTING SERIOUS airplay in the church in North America now, but its earliest proponents were over in the UK, and it was the Gospel Coalition that provided this British invasion its own *Ed Sullivan Show*. The Gospel Coalition is a group of Reformed religious leaders who maintain a high profile here in the US, and on December 3, 2015, they ran this headline on their website: "Godliness Is Not Heterosexuality."

When I read the headline, I was disappointed. You couldn't call it subtle. My wife Mary Lee commented, "They're trying to take heterosexuals down a notch, reminding people that everyone sins and the church needs to become"—lifting her arms, she made a circle—"more accepting of gays."

The headline made us wonder whom the Coalition was trying to correct? Was there a "Godliness *Is* Heterosexuality" movement we didn't know about?

Back to that British invasion. According to Google, the only place on the Internet the phrase "godliness is heterosexuality" can be found is in the writing of a pastor named Ed Shaw who serves a church in Bristol, England. Pastor Shaw says the church needs a "Godliness Is Not

Heterosexuality" movement because, "far too often in the evangelical church, godliness is heterosexuality."[1]

The piece published by the Gospel Coalition was an excerpt from an American edition of a book Pastor Shaw published over in the UK titled *The Plausibility Problem: The Church and Same-Sex Attraction*.[2] Shaw is an Anglican pastor who identifies himself as a homosexual, and his book was chosen by the Gospel Coalition as one of their editor's picks for 2015. Shaw writes:

> I was recently on a panel talking about same-sex attraction at a large Christian conference. One of the questions I was asked was a thinly veiled version of the one question many Christian parents most want to ask me: "How can I stop my children from being same-sex attracted?" or (as no one has really had the courage to put it) "How can I stop my child from becoming like you?"[3]

Given the questions asked at this conference, Shaw must have identified himself to the audience as a gay Christian. He tells us some Christian father or mother asked him how they could help their son not to "abandon the natural function of the woman" and "burn in his desire" for another man.

Pastor Shaw resents the question because it implies there's something about his life and desires that the parents don't want their son or daughter to suffer.

It's time for our biblical test. Since Scripture lists a number of sexual perversions together in its condemnation of them, let's insert one of those perversions into Pastor Shaw's statement and see how it works out.

Let's say, instead of announcing to conference attendees that he was a gay Christian, Pastor Shaw had announced he was a "pedophile Chris-

---

1. Ed Shaw, "Godliness Is Not Heterosexuality," *Christian Living* (blog), The Gospel Coalition, accessed August 4, 2017, https://www.thegospelcoalition.org/article/godliness-is-not-heterosexuality.

2. Published in the US under the title *Same-Sex Attraction and the Church: The Surprising Plausibility of the Celibate Life* (Downers Grove, IL: InterVarsity Press, 2015).

3. Shaw, *Same-Sex Attraction and the Church*, 95. Compare Shaw, "Godliness Is Not Heterosexuality."

tian," stipulating that he didn't have sex with, or even touch, children. If that had been the case, the text on the Gospel Coalition's website might have read:

> I was recently on a panel talking about <u>attraction to children</u> at a large Christian conference. One of the questions I was asked was a thinly veiled version of the one question that many Christian parents most want to ask me: "How can I stop my children from <u>wanting to have sex with children</u>?" or (as no one has really had the courage to put it) "How can I stop my child from becoming like you?"[4]

Changing the sexual sin from sodomy to pedophilia clarifies things, doesn't it? Every sane Christian father and mother would want to help their children flee from any sexual desire for children. Christian fathers and mothers don't want their children to grow up to identify themselves publicly as a man who has abandoned the natural function of the woman to burn in his desire for little children, regardless of whether or not their son adds that he is committed to never actually bedding any children. If some man at a large Christian conference identified himself as a "pedophile Christian," attendees would wonder what the conference planning committee had been thinking putting such a man on any panel taking questions about anything at all.

Pastor Shaw might continue (still in his own words, except for changing the sin from homosexuality to pedophilia):

> It's a revealing question. The number of times I've been asked it (always in roundabout ways) demonstrates how great a fear it is for many Christian parents—to raise a child that might be sexually attracted <u>to children</u>. It's not something that they want to have to share in the Christmas letter in years to come—either openly or by what's clearly left unsaid. The great hope is that they will be able to write of happy marriages, numerous grandchildren and continued involvement in a good evangelical church. They don't want to have to say instead that a child is <u>a pedophile</u> . . . and that their son or

---

4. Our replacements underlined.

daughter is now part of some <u>pedophile</u>-affirming church (if any church at all). What they want from me is a few simple steps they can take to stop that from happening. . . .

Why the paranoia (a word honestly used by a Christian parent asking me this question)? It's because, in the evangelical church, godliness is <u>wanting to have sex with adults</u> and no one can really grasp how <u>attraction to children</u> and godliness could ever exist together.[5]

Try to imagine the Gospel Coalition inviting a "pedophile Christian" to speak at one of their conferences. Imagine them running an excerpt from a book written by a "pedophile Christian" on their website—an excerpt in which the pedophile complains that he's tired of the stigma fathers and mothers put on him when he speaks at Christian conferences.

It's incomprehensible.

Now, back to the Gospel Coalition's headline, "Godliness Is Not Heterosexuality."

Maybe evangelicals in the UK have a different experience, but speaking as evangelicals in the States (and Germany), we've never run into anyone writing or preaching that "godliness is heterosexuality." It's such an inane thing to think, let alone say.

Godliness is heterosexuality? Hasn't every heterosexual man who knows God struggled against sinful heterosexual lusts of his flesh?

Godliness is contentment and self-control. It is not concupiscence. It is not the lust of the flesh and the lust of the eyes. Lust has always dogged most heterosexuals' experience of their own heterosexuality—including righteous Job, who said, "I have made a covenant with my eyes; how then could I gaze at a virgin?"[6]

Godliness is heterosexuality?

Uh, no. This sort of simplistic thought is not that of any sane Christian man whose sexual desire, by God's grace, *is* entirely heterosexual. Straight Christians are not sitting around patting ourselves on the

---

5. Shaw, *Same-Sex Attraction and the Church*, 95–96. Our replacements underlined. Compare Shaw, "Godliness Is Not Heterosexuality."

6. Job 31:1.

back because we're straight. It's the rare man who takes pride in his heterosexuality anymore. Twenty years ago my friend who was a public-school teacher in a Chicago suburb told me gay was hip, and since then everyone's been "living out." We have gay actors, gay Republicans, gay NBA players, gay authors, gay defensive linemen, gay cowboys, gay pastors . . .

In fact, anyone who tries to rain on the gay rainbow will be tarred and feathered on Facebook and Twitter, or bankrupted by some federal judge. This is not a world in which Christian Joes or Janes are walking around congratulating themselves that "godliness is heterosexuality."

Sure, it's understandable how Pastor Shaw could begin to resent heterosexuals. It's understandable that he could grow bitter against the Christian man who has not abandoned the natural function of the woman to burn in his desire for another man. He may well resent the Christian man who has turned from burning in his desire for another man to loving the woman God made him to desire. He surely would not find it easy to watch other men in church who have repented of gay lust and sodomy, and who have obeyed Scripture by marrying rather than burning;[7] men who now have the joy of godly heterosexual marriages and are, with their wives, raising up a godly seed for God. It's understandable that a Christian man who has spent years single and burning in his desire for other men might grow weary and tell the church he is a "gay Christian" and proud of it—adding that "godliness is not heterosexuality!"

Why has the Gospel Coalition jumped on this bandwagon? Did we need another defense of homosexuality at the expense of heterosexuality? Was there a heterosexualist movement springing up in the church that gay Christians found threatening? Did the men of the Coalition really think now was the time to mount a campaign against the privileging of heterosexuality? And if so, did they think it best for this campaign to be led by a gay pastor who resents the way Christian fathers and mothers have treated him? A gay pastor who is bitter about his residual feelings of shame about his gayness in the church? A gay pastor who is angry at being asked by Christian parents how they can help their sons avoid effeminacy?

---

7. "It is better to marry than to burn." 1 Corinthians 7:9.

Context is everything in interpreting the sentences and words of Scripture. Context also matters in coming to understand the sentences and words of the Coalition's headline, "Godliness Is Not Heterosexuality."

For two decades, homosexualists have been hard at work gaining the sympathy of middle America. Unsurprisingly, a growing number of evangelical church members want the church to make its peace with this leviathan that is leaving the evangelical establishment looking clueless, brain-dead, passé, insensitive, outmoded, dowdy, fusty, musty, unloving, and just plain stupid.

Just a few weeks before the *Obergefell* ruling, the Pew Research Center announced its latest figures on the support of homosexual marriage, categorized by age or generation. The numbers were clear. There is now an overwhelming support for homosexuality and homosexual marriage across North America, but what was even more noteworthy in the Pew results was the rapidity of the change in convictions.

For instance, take Millennials (those born after 1980): in 2005, 49 percent supported homosexual marriage, but just ten years later the support had grown to 70 percent—a gain of more than 20 percent.[8]

In a nation in which 70 percent of its citizens claim Christian faith,[9] such a reversal of conviction about such a foundational moral command of Scripture is astounding. Pastors would have to be quite obtuse not to see the importance of this change for our teaching, preaching, and pastoral care. If we're going to continue to have the ears and hearts of our families and congregations, we must realize our credibility problem is real and growing. And who better to help us adjust to present realities than a gay Christian pastor from the United Kingdom who wrote the book on it, titled *The Plausibility Problem: The Church and Same-Sex Attraction*?

The men of the Gospel Coalition saw the dwindling support for Scripture's condemnation of homosexuality and felt it was time to distance themselves from their former position. They didn't want evangeli-

---

8. "Changing Attitudes on Gay Marriage," Pew Research Center, June 26, 2017, http://www.pewforum.org/fact-sheet/changing-attitudes-on-gay-marriage/.

9. "America's Changing Religious Landscape," Pew Research Center, May 12, 2015, http://www.pewforum.org/2015/05/12/americas-changing-religious-landscape/.

cal Millennials to judge them hardline. Kinder, gentler was needed and the Gospel Coalition had it covered.

But in declaring that "godliness is not heterosexuality," they were too cute by half. Which is to say, they lied.

Godliness is living as the sex God made us and loving the opposite sex, and this is what normal people mean when they speak of "heterosexuality."

Brothers and sisters, we must be done with hiding God's truth behind mincing phrases and half-truths. We may be so self-deceived that we can't see it ourselves, but everyone else sees and understands our shame at Scripture's repeated condemnations of androgyny, effeminacy, sodomy, and lesbianism.

Let others who aren't ashamed of Jesus and His words speak for Him. Let them love sinners and call them to repentance and faith. Let them preach the Gospel clearly and boldly, without such shameful equivocation.

May God help us to follow the clarity and boldness of the Apostle Paul who described his preaching this way:

> I was not vacillating when I intended to do this, was I? Or what I purpose, do I purpose according to the flesh, so that with me there will be yes, yes and no, no at the same time? But as God is faithful, our word to you is not yes and no. For the Son of God, Christ Jesus, who was preached among you by us—by me and Silvanus and Timothy—was not yes and no, but is yes in Him. For as many as are the promises of God, in Him they are yes; therefore also through Him is our Amen to the glory of God through us.[10]

---

10. 2 Corinthians 1:17–20.

He created them male and female, and He blessed them and
named them Man in the day when they were created.

Genesis 5:2

CHAPTER 7

ERROR 4

The "Sexual Orientation" Error

THE BIBLE SAYS GOD "CREATED THEM MALE AND FE-
male." Jesus repeated this statement: "Have you not read that He who
created them from the beginning made them male and female?"[1]

Male.

Female.

Two sexes only. One for the other.

Yet now, some within the church have begun to claim there is something more to sexual identity than male and female. They call this third
category of sexuality "sexual orientation," telling Christians this third
rail exists independent of the male or female God made us from our
beginning—at the moment of our conception. They are abandoning
God's two for the mélange of LGBTQ "gender identities."

Take, for example, Dr. Albert Mohler who serves as president of
Southern Baptist Theological Seminary in Louisville, Kentucky. For
quite a while Dr. Mohler has had high visibility as a defender of biblical
sexuality. Recently, though, Dr. Mohler repudiated his prior positions
on a matter homosexuals have put at the top of their revolutionary
agenda—sexual orientation.

---

1. Matthew 19:4.

On October 28, 2014, Dr. Mohler gave a speech apologizing for his past denial of homosexual orientation:

> One of the things we should not be embarrassed to say is that we are learning. One of the embarrassments that I have to bear is that I have written on some of these issues now for nearly thirty years, and at a couple of points I have to say, "I got that wrong," and we have to go back and correct it, correct it by Scripture.
>
> Now early in this controversy I felt it quite necessary, in order to make clear the Gospel, to deny anything like a sexual orientation, and speaking at an event for the National Association of Evangelicals twenty-something years ago, I made that point. I repent of that.[2]

A couple weeks later, Dr. Mohler tried to calm the waters by issuing a blog post explaining the conference and what he had said there:

> I recently addressed a major national conference on "The Gospel, Homosexuality, and the Future of Marriage" held by the Ethics and Religious Liberty Commission of the Southern Baptist Convention. As expected, the conference was one of the most responsible and edifying meetings yet held of Christians concerned about these issues. This is exactly what would be expected of the ERLC and its leadership. The conference was both helpful and historic. I had the honor of delivering the opening keynote address entitled "Aftermath: Ministering in a Post-Marriage Culture."[3]

In his keynote address, Mohler made these claims:

> I believe that a biblical-theological understanding, a robust biblical

---

2. Albert Mohler, "Aftermath: Ministering in a Post-Marriage Culture" (keynote address, *The Gospel, Homosexuality, and the Future of Marriage*, national conference of the Ethics & Religious Liberty Commission of the Southern Baptist Convention, Nashville, TN, October 27–29, 2014), video, 29:22, October 28, 2014, http://erlc.com/resource-library/event-messages/aftermath-ministering-in-a-post-marriage-culture-albert-mohler.

3. Mohler, "Sexual Orientation and the Gospel of Jesus Christ," on Albert Mohler's official website, November 13, 2014, http://www.albertmohler.com/2014/11/13/sexual-orientation-and-the-gospel-of-jesus-christ/.

theology, would point to us that human sexual, affective profiles—
who we are sexually—is far more deeply rooted than just the will—
if that were so easy!

But Genesis 3 explains that, helps us to understand that this
complex of same-sex challenges coming to us is something that is
deeply rooted in the biblical story itself, and something that we need
to take with far greater seriousness than we have taken it in the past,
understanding that that requires a far more robust Gospel response
than anything the church has come up with heretofore.[4]

Apparently, the conference was "historic" because it began to lead
the church into a new and "far more robust Gospel response" to homosexuality "than anything the church has come up with" over its 2,000-
year history.

Listening to the address, we got the sense that Dr. Mohler realized
he'd set some of his listeners' teeth on edge and tried to nuance his
sweeping condemnation of the church's witness concerning homosexuality:

I don't believe the Christian church has misread Scripture for two
millennia. I don't believe that there was information lacking to the
Holy Spirit that would have changed the meaning of these texts,
information that's now available to us.[5]

So what does Mohler believe? In his follow-up blog post, he writes:

Put simply, most people experiencing a same-sex attraction tell of
discovering it within themselves at a very early age, certainly within
early puberty. As they experience it, a sexual attraction or interest
simply "happens," and they come to know it. . . .

The concept of sexual orientation is not only helpful, it is in
some sense essential. Even those who argue against its existence
have to describe and affirm something tantamount to it. There is a

---

4. Mohler, "Aftermath," 29:54.
5. Ibid., 30:44.

pattern of sexual interest and attraction that is discovered in early adolescence. It is not something that is, in itself, freely chosen. . . .

. . . Our biblically-informed understanding of sexual orientation will chasten us from having any confidence that there is any rescue from same-sex attraction to be found in any secular approach, therapy, or treatment. Christians know that the only remedy for sin is the atonement of Christ and the gift of salvation. The only hopeful answer to sin, in any form, is the Gospel of Christ.[6]

Here's how Bryan Fischer, graduate of Stanford University and Dallas Theological Seminary, and host of the radio show *Focal Point*, responded to Dr. Mohler's 2014 statement:

I'm not sure there is any way to interpret Dr. Mohler's statement other than that he believes, along with Lady Gaga, that homosexuals are "born that way."

Now if people are "born that way," then it's like hair color or eye color. It's not something you can change. Perhaps it is something you can control, but not something that you can change. Thus, it's a logical extension of Dr. Mohler's position to write that Dr. Mohler was repenting of the thought that it is possible for homosexual sinners to change their orientation.

Now if Dr. Mohler does believe that individuals can be born that way, he is certainly wrong. Despite decades of fruitless research, no gay gene has ever been identified. Even pro-homosexual researchers have thrown in the towel. Research done on identical twins reveals that the concordance rate for homosexuality, which should be 100% if homosexuality is genetically determined, is only between five and seven percent.

If Dr. Mohler is not saying homosexuals are born that way, then what exactly does he mean by the term "orientation"? And does he believe that an individual's sexuality can be re-oriented to bring it in line with God's design for humanity?

---

6. Mohler, "Sexual Orientation and the Gospel."

These are straightforward questions. However, rather than answering them, Dr. Mohler demanded through his spokesman that Pastor Fischer retract what he had written.[7]

The truth is, if Dr. Mohler *had* answered Pastor Fischer's question and clearly denied that some people are "born that way," his recent statements about the existence of homosexual orientation would have become meaningless.

Following this reversal on homosexual orientation, Dr. Mohler changed other parts of his approach to homosexuality. He abandoned his support for conversion therapy, calling on Christian pastors to stop providing it.[8] Also, Dr. Mohler's Gospel Coalition has begun promoting the gay Christian lobby LivingOut.org[9] and ran a headline on its website claiming that "godliness is not heterosexuality."[10]

This change of strategy arrived at the same time a tsunami of support for gays, lesbians, and gay marriage washed across North America. The Supreme Court took the occasion to issue their *Obergefell* ruling which legalized homosexual marriage.

There wasn't a pastor in the country who missed the new spirit sweeping our land. Past firmness had to go. If Christians were going to continue to have a voice in our national conversation, we were going to have to finesse our previous positions.

It seemed like good strategy to back off everything but the fitting together of body parts. Thus was birthed the new sweet spot of Christian witness in the face of gay liberation. We would still say that homosexual intercourse was forbidden, but we'd now endorse homosexual orientation and condemn any counseling that seeks to lead souls away from it.

Homosexualists celebrated these changes. In an open letter to Dr. Mohler published on *HuffPost Gay Voices* in October 2015, homosexualist Derek Penwell wrote:

---

7. Bryan Fischer, "The curious case of Dr. Albert Mohler," OneNewsNow, December 2, 2014, https://www.onenewsnow.com/perspectives/bryan-fischer/2014/12/02/the-curious-case-of-dr-albert-mohler. Fischer reproduces his Twitter exchange with Mohler's chief spokesman James A. Smith.

8. See chapter 8.

9. See chapter 10.

10. See chapter 6.

I want to congratulate you on being such a visible illustration of the progress we've made in our understanding of LGBTQ people and the dignity their lives should rightfully be afforded. . . .

. . . I mean, think about it: when even Al Mohler is embarrassed to talk about "reparative therapy" in straightforward terms everyone understands, it means that cultural standards are evolving toward greater hospitality to our LGBTQ sisters and brothers. . . .

Put more simply, when someone as anti-LGBTQ as you've been is afraid of looking as anti-LGBTQ as you used to, that's monumentally huge, dude! You're helping us show the world that becoming less bigoted and more inclusive is actually possible. I can't even tell you. Congratulations! And thank you for doing your part![11]

A similar response came from Chelsen Vicari of Washington DC's conservative think tank, the Institute on Religion & Democracy:

I was very surprised by Dr. Mohler's changing tone. And I was very thankful that he took time during his speech to actually confess that he had gotten sexual orientation wrong earlier in his career and that he is willing to say that there are individuals who are born with an innate sexual attraction to the same gender.[12]

Listening to Dr. Mohler, one would expect him to make some reference to the longstanding division in the gay world between the essentialist and the social constructivist views on homosexuality. Homosexual orientation continues to be debated among gays and lesbians, and many of them say there's no such thing. On one side of the conflict are those who say there are homosexual ways of acting and living and copulating, but there are no homosexuals. These are the social construc-

11. Derek Penwell, "An Open Letter to Al Mohler on Taking a Transparently Meaningless Stand on Reparative Therapy," *HuffPost Gay Voices*, October 6, 2015, accessed February 1, 2016, http://www.huffingtonpost.com/derek-penwell/an-open-letter-to-al-mohl_b_8253224.html.

12. Quoted in Charlie Butts, "Where are Southern Baptist leaders headed re: homosexuality?" OneNewsNow, October 30, 2014, http://www.onenewsnow.com/church/2014/10/30/where-are-southern-baptist-leaders-headed-re-homosexuality#.VHxkIzCJOuZ.

tivists. On the other side are those who say there are homosexual ways of acting and living and copulating, and these ways are characteristic of the homosexual. These are the essentialists.

Here's how scholar Thomas Hubbard summarizes the division:

> The field of Gay Studies has, virtually since its inception, been divided between "essentialists," those who believe in an archetypal pattern of same-gender attraction that is universal, transhistorical, and transcultural, and "social constructivists," those who hold that patterns of sexual preference manifest themselves with different significance in different societies and that no essential identity exists between practitioners of same-gender love in, for instance, ancient Greece and postindustrial Western society.[13]

This debate has been going on for decades and is illustrated by this excerpt from an interview with bisexual author Gore Vidal, published by *Fag Rag*:

FAG RAG. You've said that you didn't think that anyone was a homosexual.

GORE VIDAL. I've always said it was just an adjective. It's not a noun, though it's always used as a noun.[14]

Vidal affirms there are homosexual sensibilities, homosexual aesthetics, and homosexual acts, but he denies there are any homosexuals. A man may have homosexual sex, but having homosexual sex doesn't make him a homosexual because there is no such thing as a homosexual. And if there is no such thing as a homosexual, the notion of homosexual orientation itself makes no sense.

Note carefully that a significant part of the homosexualist world denies the existence of any "essential" homosexual "identity." Embracing

---

13. *Homosexuality in Greece and Rome: A Sourcebook of Basic Documents* (Berkeley: University of California Press, 2003), 2.

14. *Fag Rag* (Winter/Spring 1974), reprinted in *Conversations with Gore Vidal*, ed. Richard Peabody and Lucinda Ebersole (Jackson: University Press of Mississippi, 2005), 17.

homosexual orientation necessarily means to endorse one camp within the divided homosexualist world.[15]

But why would Christians do that? Our Lord said,

Have you not read that He who created them from the beginning made them male and female?

When we declare in favor of homosexual orientation, we stake out a third sexual category that's a function of a man's psychological composition and identity—not his body parts. Those who believe in this third category claim that the hardwiring of God's sexual bifurcation of mankind into male and female isn't sufficient to encompass man's experience of sexuality.

Of course, no Christian in his right mind would disagree with Dr. Mohler's statement that "the only hopeful answer to sin, of any kind, is the Gospel of Christ." But note how his statement begs the question: What is the Gospel of Jesus Christ for those who claim to be the in this third sexual category possessing something they call the "homosexual orientation"?

If we all agree that Jesus is not calling us to embrace effeminacy and men lying with males (nor women lying with females), why would we turn around and affirm these sinners' justification of their sins by claiming they were made with a "homosexual orientation"? Why bother objecting to the perverse acts that trample on the genitalia God gave us and calls us to live in accordance with, then turn around and endorse the perverse identity that tramples on the male mind and heart God gave us and calls us to live in accordance with?

Instead, we connive at this wickedness by speaking sympathetically about how God gave such souls their homosexual orientation and they should not think it will change because it was there in them from the

15. For a better understanding of the division among homosexualists between essentialists and social constructivists, see David M. Munsey, "The Love That Need Not Name Its Speaker," https://www.ibiblio.org/gaylaw/issue3/munsey.html; John D. DeLamater and Janet Shibley Hyde, "Essentialism vs. Social Constructionism in the Study of Human Sexuality," *The Journal of Sex Research* 35, no. 1 (1998): 10–18.

very beginning. That their homosexual orientation is merely one more aspect of the brokenness we all suffer in this fallen world.

Before we declare how robust and historic it is for us to announce that homosexuals are born with a homosexual orientation, let's look at the secular research on the subject.

A recent survey of the literature, titled "Sexuality and Gender: Findings from the Biological, Psychological, and Social Sciences," addresses the question of whether people are "born that way" as follows:

> The most commonly accepted view in popular discourse we mentioned above—the "born that way" notion that homosexuality and heterosexuality are biologically innate or the product of very early developmental factors—has led many non-specialists to think that homosexuality or heterosexuality is in any given person unchangeable and determined entirely apart from choices, behaviors, life experiences, and social contexts. However, as the following discussion of the relevant scientific literature shows, this is not a view that is well-supported by research.
>
> . . . Any attempt to infer a stable, innate, and fixed identity from a complex and often shifting mélange of inner fantasies, desires, and attractions—sexual, romantic, aesthetic, or otherwise—is fraught with difficulties.[16]

Concerning the idea of a young man attempting to find the answer to the enigmatic question, "Does this mean I'm gay?" the study goes on to say,

> Current research from the biological, psychological, and social sciences suggests that this question, at least as it is framed, makes little sense. As far as science can tell us, there is nothing "there" for this young man to discover—no fact of nature to uncover or to find buried within himself.[17]

---

16. Mayer and McHugh, "Sexuality and Gender," 26, 57.
17. Ibid., 57.

Citing secular studies can only get us so far in this debate, but it's worth noting that the secular scientific evidence does not back up Mohler's reversal and new assertion that there is such a thing as homosexual orientation.

Turning to Scripture, let's note how Jesus led the Samaritan woman to repentance. He didn't avoid or excuse her adulteries. Rather, He exposed her sin in all its horror, and this was used by the Holy Spirit to turn this dear woman to faith and repentance.

Plain speaking did not turn the Samaritan woman off to Jesus or His Gospel. Naming her guilt and shame was no obstruction to her repentance. Just the opposite. Remember what she said to the other villagers: "Come, see a man who told me all the things that I have done; this is not the Christ, is it?"[18]

The Samaritan woman was a sexual sinner—an adulteress. Jesus exposed her sin, and she repented. If, with Al Mohler, we turn and embrace the legitimacy of homosexual orientation, will we present the Gospel to homosexuals in the same way Jesus presented His Gospel to this adulteress?

To see why not, let's apply our biblical test. In Scripture, the sin of homosexuality appears alongside incest.[19] Suppose we argued for an "incestuous orientation." Let's try it out by changing Dr. Mohler's statements above only at the naming of the sin:

> Put simply, most people experiencing <u>an incestuous</u> attraction tell of discovering it within themselves at a very early age, certainly within early puberty. As they experience it, <u>an incestuous</u> attraction or interest simply "happens," and they come to know it. . . .
>
> . . . The concept of <u>an incestuous</u> orientation is not only helpful, it is in some sense essential. Even those who argue against its existence have to describe and affirm something tantamount to it. There is a pattern of <u>incestuous</u> interest and attraction that is discovered in early adolescence. It is not something that is, in itself, freely chosen. . . .
>
> Our biblically-informed understanding of <u>incestuous</u> orienta-

---

18. John 4:29.
19. For example, see Leviticus 20:11–14.

tion will chasten us from having any confidence that there is any rescue from <u>a sexual attraction to one's siblings</u> to be found in any secular approach, therapy, or treatment. Christians know that the only remedy for sin is the atonement of Christ and the gift of salvation. The only hopeful answer to sin, in any form, is the Gospel of Christ.[20]

It doesn't work, does it? The statement becomes ridiculous, but only because our culture still views incest with disgust.

If we say no to an "incestuous orientation," why say yes to a "homosexual orientation"?

If the whole point of homosexual orientation is to get Christians to understand how early the onset and intractable the temptation of homosexual sin is, we could all agree. There are many sins that have an early onset and a terrible tenacity.

But if the onset and tenacity of the sin is the heart of our concern, we could stop talking about "homosexual orientation," and speak instead about "homosexual temptation."

"Homosexual *temptation*" brings back the very moral judgment "homosexual *orientation*" so preciously works to exclude. If our goal in coming out in support of "homosexual orientation" is to be perceived as a kinder, gentler sort of Christian, "temptation" blows our cover because it returns homosexuality to the arena of moral judgment and sin.

In a short 2015 book by Southern Baptist theologians Denny Burk and Heath Lambert titled *Transforming Homosexuality*, the authors address this issue. They write:

When sexual desire or attraction fixes on any kind of non-marital erotic activity, it falls short of the glory of God and is, by definition, sinful.[21]

They drive the point home with this statement by nineteenth-century Princeton theologian, Charles Hodge:

20. Our replacements underlined.
21. Denny Burk and Heath Lambert, *Transforming Homosexuality: What the Bible Says about Sexual Orientation and Change* (P&R Publishing, 2015), 48.

All Christian churches receive the doctrines of original sin and regeneration in a form which involves not only the principle that dispositions, as distinguished from acts, may have a moral character, but also that such character belongs to them whether they be innate, acquired, or infused. It is, therefore, most unreasonable to assume the ground that a man can be responsible only for his voluntary acts, or for their subjective effects, when our own consciousness, the universal judgment of men, the word of God, and the Church universal, so distinctly assert the contrary.[22]

This is why, in the end, Burk and Lambert fundamentally question the concept of homosexual orientation:

For these reasons, same-sex orientation as an identity category is problematic. From a Christian perspective, it invites us to embrace fictional identities that go directly against God's revealed purposes for his creation.[23]

To conclude this chapter, we must point to an important tenet of the homosexual-orientation argument. This is the claim that homosexuals have no choice. Instead, people allegedly "experience a same-sex attraction" or "discover it within themselves." It arrives "in early adolescence" and "is not something that is, in itself, freely chosen."

Such arguments serve to minimize, if not deny, the moral agency of those with the "homosexual orientation."

Examine the claim that homosexual orientation comes at a very early age, noting the accompanying denial that homosexual orientation is freely chosen, and we see the project more clearly. In the end, claiming that it is homosexual orientation that leads to homosexual sin comes down to blaming nature, and thus nature's God.

In his *Institutes*, John Calvin warns against our constant attempts to transfer the blame for our sin to God:

We must guard against singling out only those natural evils of man,

---

22. Ibid., 32, quoting Charles Hodge, *Systematic Theology*.
23. Ibid., 36.

lest we seem to attribute them to the Author of nature. For in this excuse, impiety thinks it has sufficient defense, if it is able to claim that whatever defects it possesses have in some way proceeded from God. It does not hesitate, if it is reproved, to contend with God Himself, and to impute to Him the fault of which it is deservedly accused. And those who wish to seem to speak more reverently of the Godhead still willingly blame their depravity on nature, not realizing that they also, although more obscurely, insult God. For if any defect were proved to inhere in nature, this would bring reproach upon Him.

Claiming that "homosexual orientation" is "experienced" rather than chosen amounts to blaming it on God. It's the difference between saying, "This is the way I am," and, "This is one of the ways I'm tempted." More than that, it insults God for, as Calvin puts it, "if any defect were proved to inhere in nature, this would bring reproach upon Him."

How should the faithful shepherd respond to men who claim the moral neutrality of homosexual orientation?

Calvin gives this counsel:

Since, then, we see the flesh panting for every subterfuge by which it thinks that the blame for its own evils may in any way be diverted from itself to another, we must diligently oppose this evil intent. Therefore we must so deal with the calamity of mankind that we may cut off every shift, and may vindicate God's justice from every accusation.[24]

---

24. John Calvin, *Institutes* 1.15.1.

As David's time to die drew near, he charged Solomon his son, saying, "I am going the way of all the earth. Be strong, therefore, and show yourself a man."

1 Kings 2:1–2

Be on the alert, stand firm in the faith, act like men, be strong.

1 Corinthians 16:13

CHAPTER 8

ERROR 5

The "Reparative Therapy" Error

"REPARATIVE THERAPY" GOES BY MANY NAMES, INCLUD-
ing "conversion therapy," "orientation therapy," and even the wordy
"sexual orientation or gender identity change efforts." Regardless of the
label, it refers to counseling that helps to heal a man's (or woman's)
sexual dysphoria to the end that his mind, heart, and body are at peace
with each other sexually.

The opposite of reparative therapy is sex-change surgery done by
surgeons who mutilate their patients' genitals in an attempt to make
them resemble the sex they aren't. Beyond the surgery are these doctors'
drugs. Reparative therapy doesn't need drugs, but sex-change surgeons
use drugs to give their male patients breasts and their female patients
facial hair.

So which of these would a reasonable person think is being criminalized across our nation right now: the counseling that helps men and
women to be the men and women God made them, or the surgery and
drugs that mutilate their manhood and womanhood?

If your guess is the counseling that helps men and women to be
the men and women God made them, you're right. The "reparative
therapy," "conversion therapy," or "orientation therapy" which is being

criminalized around the country is any counseling that helps men and women, boys and girls, who claim a homosexual orientation to embrace their heterosexual manhood or womanhood. It's that simple.

But before we get there, let's examine the recent declaration by a certain Christian seminary president and one of his professors that they oppose "reparative therapy."

> The goal of Reparative Therapy is heterosexuality. . . .
>
> This goal is not one that biblical counselors can embrace. The Bible never declares that heterosexuality is the goal of a full and contented life. . . .
>
> . . . The Holy Spirit will not give his grace to pursue goals not prescribed in Scripture.[1]

Yes, you read it right. The Holy Spirit will not bless pastors working at the request of Christian parents to help their children love and live the sex God made them, and it's because the Bible never calls us to identify with, love, and live the manhood or womanhood God made us.

We've spent decades ministering to souls who grew up in our sexually debauched world, many of those years as pastors in a sexually debauched community dominated by a major public research university. And we have never heard anyone—not even the most rabid feminist or godless sodomite—say anything as inane as suggesting that Scripture doesn't command and commend heterosexuality.

Yet the sexual revolutionaries are demanding that Christians agree to the criminalization of counseling that condemns homosexuality and commends heterosexuality. Many church leaders feel pressure to raise the white flag, but how to pull it off without everyone seeing the fear in our eyes and trembling of our hands?

Maybe all it will take for us to get ahead of this tidal wave of opposition is for us to say we oppose the same thing the homosexuals oppose. So let's reverse ourselves on homosexual orientation and say it's a real deal, then reverse ourselves on heterosexual orientation and

---

1. Heath Lambert, "What's Wrong with Reparative Therapy?" Association of Certified Biblical Counselors, November 16, 2014, https://biblicalcounseling.com/2014/11/whats-wrong-with-reparative-therapy/.

say we repudiate any counselor or pastor who works with any soul to embrace it.

Feeling the need to batten down the hatches on their bald-faced lie, these men then take the name of the Holy Spirit in vain by declaring, "The Holy Spirit will not give his grace to pursue goals not prescribed in Scripture." What higher authority could you appeal to in order to scare the simple away from counseling that leads homosexuals to embrace the heterosexual identity God gave them?

We'll return to the response of Christian leaders. But first, let's examine exactly what we are facing from the world as it attempts to outlaw this practice.

What unbelievers (and increasing numbers of believers) are committed to, sexually, is the inalienable right of every boy and girl, man and woman, to choose their "gender identity" without respect to the sex God made them. This is the simple reason our nation is in the process of criminalizing sexual orientation therapy everywhere. Christian counseling that calls boys and girls, men and women, to accept and live the sex God made them is a stake through the heart of our national gods.

By the end of 2016, Oregon, Illinois, New York, New Jersey, Vermont, DC, and California, as well as Seattle, Miami Beach, Miami, West Palm Beach, Pittsburg, Toledo, and Cincinnati had laws against reparative therapy, with legislation pending in many other cities and states. At this early stage, bans are limited to the treatment of minors, but this will change.

Cincinnati's ordinance against orientation conversion therapy reads:

WHEREAS, the City of Cincinnati has a compelling interest in protecting the physical and psychological well-being of minors, including lesbian, gay, bisexual and transgender youth and in protecting its minors against exposure to serious harms caused by sexual orientation change efforts . . .

BE IT ORDAINED by the Council of the City of Cincinnati, State of Ohio: Section 1. That the Council hereby finds that being lesbian, gay, bisexual or transgender is not a disease, disorder, illness, deficiency, or shortcoming. . . .

"Sexual orientation or gender identity change efforts" means conversion therapy, reparative therapy or any other practices by mental health professionals that seek to change an individual's sexual orientation or gender identity, including efforts to change behaviors or gender expressions, or to eliminate or reduce sexual or romantic attractions or feelings toward individuals of the same sex . . . .

No mental health professional shall engage, within the geographic boundaries of the City of Cincinnati, in sexual orientation or gender identity change efforts with a minor, without regard to whether the mental health professional is compensated or receives any form of remuneration for his or her services . . . .

Whoever violates Section 769-3 shall be subject to a civil fine of $200.00. Each day in violation constitutes a separate offense.[2]

Snopes.com defends Cincinnati's law by claiming it does not make it illegal for a Christian counselor to read the Bible to a client.[3]

Snopes lies.

Nowhere does the code grant any exception to Christian counselors, nor does it contain any exemption for the reading of the Word of God. Thus, Christian counselors who read their religion's condemnations of effeminacy, sodomy, and lesbianism to a minor with sexual dysphoria or same-sex attraction are breaking the law and risk being assessed a fine of $5,000 per month and the loss of their license to practice.

Theoretically, these laws haven't yet banned Leviticus, Romans, or 1 Corinthians from being read from the pulpit of a church in the privacy of the church's sanctuary Sunday mornings, but a growing list of states and cities have now made it a criminal act for Christian counselors to call children to listen to Scripture and obey God by living faithful to the manhood or womanhood He gave them.

That's the issue we're facing. Now back to the Christian response to it.

On October 5, 2015, the Southern Baptist Theological Seminary

---

2. Cincinnati, Ohio, Municipal Ordinance No. 373-2015, http://city-egov.cincinnati-oh.gov /Webtop/ws/council/public/child/Blob/43697.pdf?m=1&w=doc_no%3D%27201501430%27. See also Cincinnati Municipal Code § 769.

3. "Biblical Distortions," *Snopes*, December 8, 2015, http://www.snopes.com/will-quoting-the -bible-be-made-illegal/.

in Louisville, Kentucky, was hosting a national conference of the Association of Certified Biblical Counselors (ACBC), and a group of forty homosexuals calling themselves the Fairness Campaign picketed the seminary campus. The protesters carried signs that read, "Love Needs No Cure," and, "Conversion Therapy Kills."[4]

Southern's president, Dr. Albert Mohler, and one of its faculty members (also serving as ACBC's executive director) called a press conference to tell the media that these protesters had misunderstood them. Both Southern and ACBC are opposed to reparative therapy, they told the reporters.[5]

Dr. Mohler and ACBC's executive director seemed to be in agreement with Cincinnati's city fathers who declared that "being lesbian, gay, bisexual or transgender is not a disease, disorder, illness, deficiency, or shortcoming." They were making common cause with them in denouncing therapists and pastoral counselors who "seek to change an individual's sexual orientation or gender identity, including efforts to change behaviors or gender expressions, or to eliminate or reduce sexual or romantic attractions or feelings toward individuals of the same sex."

Across the nation, this is the rationale being used to criminalize the reparative therapy these men repudiated at their press conference.

People say that sexual orientation counseling kills. Remember the signs the protesters were carrying?

"Love Needs No Cure."

"Conversion Therapy Kills."

As state legislators and city councils around the country pass laws criminalizing sexual orientation therapy, this protest (and the response to it) is a straightforward attempt to stop Christians from calling gays and lesbians to flee their sin. Once more, let us put it plainly: those writing and passing these laws are criminalizing any call to repentance. What they are opposing is the very ministry of the Apostle Paul which allowed him to write this to the Christians in Corinth:

---

4. "Activists protest Seminary's conference on homosexuality," *Wave 3 News*, last modified October 12, 2015, http://www.wave3.com/story/30191568/southern-seminary-acbc-refute-claims-it-promotes-reparative-therapy-for-gays.

5. "Reparative therapy criticized by Southern Baptist theologian," AP News, October 5, 2015, https://apnews.com/260d8379ea7c49f98ff01b1a29fc0ebl/reparative-therapy-criticized-southern-baptist-theologian.

Or do you not know that the unrighteous will not inherit the kingdom of God? Do not be deceived; neither fornicators, nor idolaters,
nor adulterers, nor effeminate, nor homosexuals, nor thieves, nor
the covetous, nor drunkards, nor revilers, nor swindlers, will inherit
the kingdom of God. *Such were some of you; but you were washed, but
you were sanctified, but you were justified in the name of the Lord Jesus
Christ and in the Spirit of our God.*[6]

Council members, state legislators, and protesters against reparative
therapy are not trying to keep members of the helping professions from
providing therapy that delves into their counselee or church member's
childhood. They're not trying to keep Christian ministers and pastoral
counselors from talking to church members about how they related to
other boys or girls when they reached puberty. They're not trying to
keep pastors from talking to their church members about their relationship with their siblings. They're not even trying to keep pastors from
calling people in general to repent in general and believe in Jesus Christ
for forgiveness of their sins in general.

What they are criminalizing is any counselor or pastor saying a single word that calls any effeminate, gay, lesbian, bisexual, or transsexual
to repent of being effeminate, gay, lesbian, bisexual, or transsexual. The
second the counselor does that (for now, with a minor), he has become
guilty of a crime.

In 2009, the American Psychological Association condemned sexual
orientation counseling. They passed resolutions saying homosexual orientation was not a mental illness, but completely natural and healthy.
Their resolutions condemned any work with gays to help them move
away from their homosexual orientation toward a heterosexual orientation. They declared such counsel to be abuse regardless of whether
the counsel was psychological, medical, religious, or spiritual; regardless
of whether the counsel was done by "religious professionals, religious
leaders, social groups, [or] other lay networks such as self-help groups."[7]

---

6. 1 Corinthians 6:9–11. Emphasis ours.
7. "Resolution on Appropriate Affirmative Responses to Sexual Orientation Distress and
Change Efforts," American Psychological Association, accessed August 11, 2017, http://www.apa
.org/about/policy/sexual-orientation.aspx.

Way back in 2004, Dr. Mohler was unequivocal in his condemnation of the APA's attacks upon religious freedom:

> The APA has become an organizing center for the homosexual movement. Its official website features numerous postings advocating gay rights, homosexual adoption, and same-sex marriage. Furthermore, the group ardently opposes all efforts to change sexual orientation through therapy and intervention.[8]

Dr. Mohler went on to describe the APA's attack on reparative therapy as a "totalitarian vengeance":

> The APA's policy statement, "Appropriate Therapeutic Responses to Sexual Orientation," includes a prohibition against therapies that seek to change sexual orientation. Another document published by the group condemns "reparative therapy" and "transformational ministry" intended to lead persons out of the homosexual lifestyle and into heterosexuality. The guidelines published in that document were also endorsed by the American Academy of Pediatrics, the American Association of School Administrators, the National Association of School Psychologists, the National Association of Social Workers, and the National Education Association.
>
> This represents a near total sweep for homosexual activists—and all at the expense of credible science and medicine. The fact that the National Education Association and the American Academy of Pediatrics affirmed the statement should send chills down the spine of every parent.
>
> The groups are holding to these new-found convictions with a totalitarian vengeance.

Eleven years later and in the face of the criminalization of orientation therapy sweeping across the United States, Dr. Mohler switched

---

8. "Psychologists Join the Gay Marriage Bandwagon," on Albert Mohler's official website, August 3, 2004, http://www.albertmohler.com/2004/08/03/psychologists-join-the-gay-marriage-bandwagon/.

sides, announcing he has lately come to believe in sexual orientation and now condemns orientation counseling.

This is the next front in the homosexualists' war against God, and as they accrue victories of this kind, fewer young men and women tempted by effeminacy and sodomy will have any place to turn for help.

The issue is simple. The world has determined that seeking change can only go one direction. If you want to convert from a man to a woman, straight to queer, holy to sinful, that's just fine and they will offer you all the help you want. On the other hand, if you want to repent of your sin, stop being transgender, stop being queer; if you want to submit to God's will for you by becoming more the man or woman He made you to be, they will do their best to prevent you from being helped by anybody,

But when the weak and helpless are oppressed, doesn't the compassion of Jesus Christ drive us to stand with them and give them every bit of love and help we can? Doesn't the authority of the Lord of all the earth compel us to obey God rather than man?

In drug recovery programs, the world makes a distinction between faith-based programs and other programs. Concerning the sins of effeminacy and sodomy, though, the world condemns any attempt to bring about change. It doesn't matter whether the program is faith-based or not. The world is intent on seducing souls to give themselves to this lust, and then keeping those souls in this lust's bondage.

We must never forget that Jesus declared that from the beginning God made us male and female. Thus each of us is to live in obedience to the specific sex God made us—man or woman. When at the moment of conception God made us male or female, He joined together our personhood and sexuality, and, as Jesus said, what God has joined together let no man separate.[9]

If calling men and women to turn away from homosexuality and embrace the heterosexuality God gave them is contrary to Scripture and is rebellion against the Holy Spirit, there are all kinds of souls who are thankful for our church and love her for being abused and misled and lied to by her. Matter of fact, we can't imagine how any man or woman

---

9. Matthew 19:6; Mark 10:9.

could begin to care for a homosexual without calling him or her to repudiate homosexuality and embrace heterosexuality.

This is Christian discipleship. This is pastoral care. This is protecting the sheep and leading them to green pastures and still waters. This is love.

Of course no one wants to get specific with an effeminate or sodomitic man about the vulnerabilities and besetting sins which have conspired to turn him away from God's heterosexuality to homosexuality, but if *Pilgrim's Progress* teaches us nothing else, it teaches us not to take shortcuts.

To join the world in opposition to conversion therapy is to join the world in its attack upon the goal of repentance and change for those caught in sexual sin. Contrary to what Southern's president would have us believe, his public condemnation of reparative therapy is not his way of protecting Gospel preaching or biblical counseling against the enemy of secularization.

The same day of the protest and press conference, the seminary posted an article on their website announcing they had called the press conference earlier that day "to refute the claims of the Fairness Campaign, a Louisville LGBT advocacy group alleging the conference promoted reparative therapy." The article asserted,

> Reparative therapy is a "superficial" response to homosexual and transgender change and Christian ministers must instead call all people to repentance and faith in Jesus Christ.[10]

The protesters were opposed to anybody doing the work of helping homosexuals to change, but Southern Baptist Theological Seminary announces to their constituents that it is Christian counselors and pastors they are concerned about.

We're left scratching our heads. Was King David wrong to call his

---

10. "Southern Seminary leaders underscore rejection of 'superficial' reparative therapy in response to LGBT protesters at ACBC conference," *Southern News* (blog), The Southern Baptist Theological Seminary, October 5, 2015, http://news.sbts.edu/2015/10/05/southern-seminary-leaders -underscore-rejection-of-superficial-reparative-therapy-in-response-to-lgbt-protesters-at-acbc -conference/.

son Solomon to be a man? Was the Apostle Paul wrong to call the men of the church of Corinth to act like men? This is the heart of the reparative therapy being criminalized across our nation, yet this seminary president and professor say such concerns are "superficial" and pastors should instead focus on "repentance and faith."

Note the false dichotomy. Southern's leaders speak as if a pastor can't call men to be men *while at the same time* calling them to repentance and faith in Jesus Christ. How does a Christian minister calling a man to repent of his effeminacy prevent him from also calling that man to repentance and faith in Jesus Christ? What is the effeminate man to repent of if not his effeminacy? Doesn't Scripture warn him that neither the effeminate, nor homosexuals will inherit the kingdom of God?

Jesus called the woman at the well to repent of her adultery. Was He wrong? Would it have been better if He'd steered clear of the elephant in the room and merely called this Samaritan woman to generic repentance that would not harm her self-esteem?

When Jesus got specific with the Samaritan woman about her adultery, was He being superficial and should we issue one of those after-the-fact apologies for Him? We mention an apology because the president and his professor went on to say, "The Christian church has sinned against the LGBT community by responding to this challenge in a superficial way."[11]

Take a moment to think about it. What they are confessing as sin is the call to repentance that has been the universal response of the Christian church to these sins from the time of the New Testament church to this very day!

And then, what are we to make of their condemnation of the church's call to repentance for being "superficial"?

Sadly, we must admit that, yes, the church's call to sexual sinners to repent has often been superficial, but not at all as these men imply. A superficial call to repentance is one that isn't specific about what repentance looks like.

A man's sexuality goes to the core of his being, so how can it be "superficial" to talk to him about ways he can embrace his manhood in Christ? What is "superficial" and why should we apologize for pleading

---

11. Ibid.

with him and praying for him to be healed of his sins of softness, complacency, fearfulness, masturbation, and irresponsibility?

No, the truth is the very opposite of what these men said. The truly superficial response of ministers to the effeminacy and sodomitic sins of the souls around them would be for them to announce they now believe in homosexual orientation and thus are opposed to reparative counseling that tries to change this homosexual orientation—covering up their retreat by telling their constituents they made this change because of their deep commitment to repentance and the pure simplicity of the Gospel.

For those of us called to pastoral ministry, it is a well-known vocational danger to remain superficial in our preaching and pastoral care by speaking in generalities of "following Christ," without any specificity about the sins that must be repented of. Thus maybe this is the most telling statement these two men made at their press conference:

> We call . . . disciples of the Lord Jesus Christ to live in holiness and wholeness, which is defined by obedience to him, each in our own way.[12]

So now, instead of calling those tempted by sexual sin to love and live the sex God made them, we'll call them to join us in obeying Jesus "each in our own way."

You can drive a semi through that hole.

Gay or straight, effeminate or manly, butch or feminine, adulterous or chaste, fornicator or celibate, homosexual or heterosexual—all of us together, obeying Jesus "each in our own way." Thieves, transsexuals, zoophiles, bisexuals, drunkards, lesbians, gays, and pedophiles—one big happy family together obeying Jesus "each in our own way."

Finally, these two seminary leaders brought their betrayal of the Gospel in the face of our sodomitic culture to an end:

> We don't call people to embrace heterosexuality. We call people to embrace Christian faithfulness.[13]

---

12. Ibid.
13. Ibid.

There is no conflict between calling people to embrace heterosexuality and Christian faithfulness. The two are entirely sympathetic.

Repentance and faith can't be pried loose from our personhood, which is to say our manhood and womanhood. Coming to faith and Christian discipleship are never asexual, because God made us in His own image, male and female.

Thus freedom in Christ always liberates us to better love and live our God-ordained manhood or womanhood. We come to faith through repentance from our effeminacy, sodomy, or lesbianism, and the sincerity of our repentance and faith is proven by embracing heterosexuality. It can't be otherwise. Anything less is superficial healing.

If we oppose reparative therapy, we tell the watching world that the effeminate and men who lie with males can't change, or don't need to. Where, then, is our Christian love for these sinners?

Maybe more to the point, where is our fear of God?

Such were some of you; but you were washed, but you were sanctified, but you were justified in the name of the Lord Jesus Christ and in the Spirit of our God.

1 Corinthians 6:11

CHAPTER 9

ERROR 6

The "Such Are Some of You" Error

DESIRING GOD MINISTRIES SET A FIRE AMONG ITS CON-
stituents with a March 16, 2016 post titled, "Does Same-Sex Attraction
Disqualify Someone from Ministry?"[1] Their answer to the question was
predictable:

> The Bible does not disqualify them from the ministry. Will you?

The post's first sentences indicated the way Desiring God wanted
their readers to approach the question:

> We've all seen the ever-increasing barrage of Christian posts, com-
> ments, and opinions about the LGBT movement in America. Many
> have responded with angry rebuttals and a fearful cowering . . .

Beginning with a warning against "angry rebuttals" and "fearful
cowering" seems unneeded. Desiring God's constituents aren't known

---

1. Dave Zuleger, "Does Same-Sex Attraction Disqualify Someone from Ministry?" *Desiring God,*
March 16, 2016, http://www.desiringgod.org/articles/does-same-sex-attraction-disqualify-someone
-from-ministry. Unless otherwise indicated, all quotes in this chapter are from this article.

for their anger and fear. Yet, in this particular case, the warning is wise. Readers are about to be jolted awake when Desiring God tells them they have no biblical basis to object to their church hiring a gay man to be their teenage son's youth pastor.

The body of the piece is made up of statements intended to erode readers' ability to understand and reject homosexualists' propaganda. Thus Desiring God warns supporters not to forget

> that the Bible says that the world is going to be a broken place because of sin, with all sorts of things misfiring, including same-sex and opposite-sex desires. . . .
>
> This is not an us versus them issue.

Then they take a moment to calm readers who may be getting nervous:

> Sin is serious and as a church we must take it seriously.

With that disclaimer, though, it's back to the larger task of removing sodomy's shame:

> Greed and idolatry (of any kind) sit on the same level as same-sex sexual activity.

Let's stop here a second and correct what Desiring God just said. If sins sit "on the same level," the implication is that no sin is any worse than any other.

Pastors sympathetic to the homosexualist movement have been trotting out this false teaching for decades. If a man wants to remove sodomy's shame, one effective strategy is to level all sins, claiming that every sin is the moral equivalent of every other sin.

For instance, everyone is greedy today. How do you live in a consumer society without being at least a little bit greedy, right? Tender consciences will quickly admit they struggle with greed, and right then at that point of humility and confession, out trots Desiring God with their declaration that greed sits "on the same level as sodomy."

Desiring God may say they didn't mean all sins are equal, but only that sodomites and the greedy are on "the same level" in the sense that both sins bar us from inheriting the kingdom of God. But if that's what they meant, why didn't they say so? They could have clarified what they were saying, but they didn't.

Instead, "on the same level" was left dangling there, enticingly; and we've been engaged in this battle long enough to know this enticement was no mistake. For several decades, the men trying to destroy the church's shame at sodomy have been arguing that sodomy is no more shameful than pride and greed because all sins are equal. So why hasn't this argument resulted in the church having more revulsion over the sins of pride and greed? Why has the argument, instead, only resulted in the church losing all its revulsion at the sin Desiring God now refers to preciously as "same-sex sexual activity"?

After reading Desiring God's circumlocution, some readers might have a hard time conjuring up what this "activity" actually consists of. On the other hand, Moses' description is direct and graphic: he speaks of men who "lie with a male as one lies with a female." Then he says it's an "abomination" and a "detestable act."[2] The Apostle Paul calls it "men-who-lie-with-a-male," and for over two thousand years this sin has been identified by words like "sodomy."[3]

Note that Desiring God uses the biblical names for greed and idolatry, so why not for the sin of the Sodomites?

If the project we're working on is getting the sheep to embrace gay Christian pastors, success will require breaking down and removing the sheep's biblical repugnance to sodomy passed down to them by two millennia of Christian fathers and mothers. If that's the goal, pulling in sins like greed and pride to "sit on the same level" with sodomy is perfect strategy. It's also good strategy to rename sodomy "same-sex sexual activity" and to commend it as "loving and monogamous."

Beyond their precious language, though, we return to Desiring God's declaration that greed, idolatry, and sodomy sit "on the same level."

---

2. Leviticus 18:22; 20:13.

3. See James B. De Young, "The Contributions of the Septuagint to Biblical Sanctions against Homosexuality," *Journal of the Evangelical Theological Society* 34, no. 2 (June 1991), 157–77, http://www.etsjets.org/files/JETS-PDFs/34/34-2/34-2-pp157-177_JETS.pdf.

Wrong. Not all sins are equal. Scripture says the opposite. Some sins are worse than others and one sin is the worst of all—blasphemy against the Holy Spirit.[4] The Apostle Paul also warns that sexual sin is worse than other sin because "the immoral man sins against his own body."[5]

Thus the Westminster Larger Catechism teaches:

> QUESTION 150. Are all transgressions of the law of God equally heinous in themselves, and in the sight of God?
>
> ANSWER. All transgressions of the law of God are not equally heinous; but some sins in themselves, and by reason of several aggravations, are more heinous in the sight of God than others.

So can we please be done with this lie?

Yes, the Word of God declares that men who are covetous, who are drunkards, who are effeminate, and men who lie with other men will not inherit the kingdom of God, but this is not to say that none of these sins are worse than the others. Sodomy is so very wicked that—along with child sacrifice, incest, and bestiality—it polluted the land of Canaan and caused that land to spew the Canaanites out.[6] That's what God said, but it's certainly not what is being said by Heath Lambert, Julie Rodgers, Russ Moore, Scott Sauls, Tim Keller, Al Mohler, and Ed Shaw.

After listing the effeminate and men-who-lie-with-a-male as sinners who would not inherit the kingdom of God, the Apostle Paul went on to say,

> Such were some of you; but you were washed, but you were sanctified, but you were justified in the name of the Lord Jesus Christ and in the Spirit of our God.[7]

Note he did not say, "Such *are* some of you."

There have always been men serving faithfully in the diaconate, el-

---

4. Mark 3:29; Luke 12:10.
5. 1 Corinthians 6:18–20.
6. Leviticus 18:22–25.
7. 1 Corinthians 6:11.

dership, and pastorate who have committed terrible sins in the past, yet God raised them up to be shepherds of His flock. Take the Apostle Paul, for instance: he had been a persecutor of Christ and His church. The Apostle Peter denied Christ three times, and later he was rebuked by the Apostle Paul for siding with the Judaizers. Lot committed incest, Augustine shacked up with his girlfriend, John Newton was a slaver— need we go on?

But this is what they *had* been, past tense. None of these men declared that these sins were their present identity. Augustine didn't come out of the closet and say he was a "fornicator Christian." Lot didn't come out of the closet and publicly identify himself as a man whose present desires ran toward incest, and he certainly wouldn't have sought to speak to large Christian conferences about the church's need to chill out about incestuous temptations and stop asking "incestuous Christians" how to keep their children from becoming incestuous Christians. King David repented of his adultery and murder; he didn't tell everyone "adulterous Christian" was his present identity and would remain so to his dying day. He didn't ask Desiring God to publish an article about how nasty and mean church people are to adulterous Christians, going on to tell their constituents that there's nothing wrong with adulterous Christians being pastors.

In the church of the New Testament, and across church history, it's been normal to examine candidates for church office and hear their confessions of sin. Every pastor has confessed sin himself and has heard other pastors, elders, and deacons confess their sin. If we were listening to a man's confession of sin during his examination for ordination and he said he had been a fornicator, murderer, or adulterer, we would not tell him he was disqualified any more than we would tell a man he was disqualified who said he had been effeminate, or had had sex with a man.

Rather, we would say: "Such were some of us; but we have been washed, we have been sanctified, we have been justified in the name of the Lord Jesus Christ and in the Spirit of our God."

But that's not what's going on here.

The entire "gay Christian" advocacy movement being promoted by the Gospel Coalition, Desiring God, and Living Out is not focused on reminding the church who we all used to be and how lost we were back then. These organizations are not naming men who have repented of effeminacy and sodomy, men who have been washed, sanctified, and justified in the name of Jesus by the power of the Holy Spirit. Quite the opposite: they are naming men who have *not* repented of effeminacy, and they are joining these men in their demand that the church stop calling them to be the men God made them.

It all comes down to past tense and present tense. The man who says he used to be gay isn't disqualified from ministry by that confession, although there may be some heavy lifting that needs to be done in exploring his past sodomies and the ways they could harm him, his wife and children, and the church of Jesus Christ, if he is ordained as a deacon, elder, or pastor. On the other hand, the man who says he *is* gay *is* disqualified, because gays will not inherit the kingdom of God.

Before we bring this chapter to an end, let us note carefully how Desiring God speaks of the sodomitic perversion in their article browbeating the church into accepting gay Christian pastors. Quoting 1 Corinthians 6:9–11 from their preferred English Standard Version which has deleted the sin of effeminacy, Desiring God goes on to say:

> Persisting unrepentantly in any of these sins should cause us to question our inheritance in the kingdom of God. Even loving, monogamous same-sex activity falls into this category because it falls outside of God's revealed will.

First, note how smoothly Desiring God moves from "same-sex attraction" to "same-sex activity." Remember Wheaton's Julie Rodgers? It's never a good idea to be precious with degrading passions because degrading passions treated tenderly give birth to abominations. Sadly, having started down the path of tenderness toward what God calls "degrading passions," we learn to speak tenderly of those abominations the passions give birth to. Thus Desiring God speaks ever so preciously of "loving, monogamous same-sex activity."

Second, note that word "falls." No one is active here; things just "fall." And sodomy just happens to "fall" into the list of sins which bar a man from Heaven.

Why does it bar a man from Heaven?

Because sodomy "falls outside God's revealed will." God doesn't condemn it. It merely "falls outside His revealed will." Some things fall inside and other things fall outside God's revealed will. When it comes to minimizing moral agency with regard to our pet sins, even God's moral agency in condemning sodomy must be minimized.

Third, note precisely what kind of sexual activity falls outside God's revealed will.

"Sodomy"?

No, not "sodomy," but "same-sex activity."

As in, "Have you noticed all the men gathered outside Lot's door asking Lot if it would be okay if they engage in same-sex activity with his houseguests?"

Sounds like a tea party, doesn't it?

Make no mistake about it: that is the point of such words, and words like that are always carefully considered at an organization like Desiring God.

Fourth, where are we to find "loving, monogamous" sodomy, anyway? Was that what caused God to consume Sodom with fire and brimstone? In ancient Greece, prostitutes advertised themselves by marking the soles of their sandals so they would leave "Follow Me" imprints in the dirt as they walked. But whereas female prostitutes could ply their trade until they were old, male prostitutes were no longer desirable after they began to grow body hair and a beard. Sodomy was pervasive in ancient Greece, but it was always between men and boys. Is this the "loving, monogamous same-sex activity" Desiring God is chatting about?

Was it loving and monogamous same-sex activity that coaches and players saw Jerry Sandusky committing against boys in Penn State's locker-room shower? Was it loving and monogamous same-sex activity that Roman Catholic priests committed against their altar boys? Was it loving and monogamous same-sex activity that caused the entire Castro District to die of AIDS?[8]

You might think us mean-spirited for saying that sodomy is never

---

8. The Castro District of San Francisco was decimated by the AIDS epidemic chronicled by the late Randy Shilts in his last work, *And the Band Played On*.

ever loving. But "loving sodomy" is an oxymoron, like "gay Christian" or "tender genocide."

God designed husband and wife, exclusively, to make love. Frat boy and sorority girl never make love. They hook up. Cheating husband and his secretary never make love. They commit adultery. Single man and single man never make love; they sodomize one another—and sodomizing isn't pretty.

So why does Desiring God speak of "loving, monogamous same-sex activity"?

Because they've drunk the Kool-Aid. Desiring God thinks of itself as a critical part of the work of the church's repentance for being so doggone hard on poor gaybies.

Please don't judge us harshly for speaking this way. We speak this way because we love the effeminate. We speak this way because we love sodomites.

Shame is their hope.

To them, shame is the Gospel.

It is eternal life.

And the man and his wife were both naked and were not ashamed.

Genesis 2:25

Then the eyes of both of them were opened, and they knew that they were naked; and they sewed fig leaves together and made themselves loin coverings.

They heard the sound of the LORD God walking in the garden in the cool of the day, and the man and his wife hid themselves from the presence of the LORD God among the trees of the garden.

Genesis 3:7–8

CHAPTER 10

ERROR 7
The "Living Out" Error

THIS BOOK WAS MOSTLY WRITTEN BEFORE THIS CHAP-
ter was added. Protecting sodomy's shame was the subtext to our work
exposing each of the errors dealt with in this book, but near the end
of our work, shame's hard substance came to the fore of our thinking
and it became clear we needed to bring the grace of shame out into the
open.

Though they don't say it explicitly, those promoting these errors are
working to remove sodomy's infamy and deny its degradation. Whether
it's men "living out" on their website as same-sex attracted Christians,
or men announcing that godliness is not heterosexuality, these church
leaders are unified in getting people to talk and talk and *talk* about sodomy with perfect equanimity. Without a hint of opprobrium or disgust.

They promote gays, lesbians, and the effeminate "living out" in the
church—and no blushing allowed.

The church's repudiation of sodomy's shame is the final step in the
acceptance of sodomy sweeping the world today. Germany just ap-
proved sodomitic marriage, and the vote was quick, following only an
hour of debate. Meanwhile, back in these United States, Pew Research
just released a poll showing 62 percent of Americans now support "mar-

riage equality." Break the poll down by generation and we find Millennial approval at 74 percent. Break it down by race and religion and we find Black Protestant approval at 44 percent, with white evangelical Protestants at 35 percent. The approval of the last two groups is climbing so rapidly that a few years from now more than half the souls of our congregations will think sodomite marriage is just fine.[1]

Noting these alarming trends, church leaders are in the midst of modulating the way they speak about sodomy, and the foundation of all their modulations is the repudiation of shame.

Never mind that this repudiation is directly contrary to the Word of God. God Himself ordained sodomites' and lesbians' shame. It is not the repressed and fearful man, nor is it the hater, who pronounces this sexual perversion's shame. The Living God pronounced it, and He did so to men living in times and places every bit as sexually perverse as our own.

Beyond faithfulness to the words of God, though, why speak of sodomy's shame?

Because those repenting of sodomy and lesbianism experience shame as God's grace. We have received emails thanking us for noting sodomy's shame through our word use. Those repenting of these sins thank us for helping them feel proper revulsion toward their temptation. Shame helps these precious souls flee their temptations.

The Holy Spirit's language is not hate speech, but the kindness of God that leads to repentance.

Concerning shame, it will help us keep our eye on the ball to note what our fellow elder Brian Bailey has observed: that just "like authority, matter, energy, and risk, shame can't be eliminated. It's just transferred from one place to another."

Thus Christians who condemn the shaming of sodomy and lesbianism are not actually repudiating shame. They merely transfer shame from sodomy itself to Scripture's words which condemn sodomy; from those who commit sodomy to those who by faith speak of sodomy in the language of Scripture.

---

1. "Changing Attitudes on Gay Marriage," Pew Research Center, June 26, 2017, http://www.pewforum.org/fact-sheet/changing-attitudes-on-gay-marriage/.

So, for instance, this past week a pastor rebuked an elder of our acquaintance for publicly stating that "sodomy" is an "abomination." The elder was defending a Christian institution under public attack for stating in its policies that homosexual practice is sin, and in the course of his defense he pointed out that the institution is Christian, and therefore under the authority of God's Word which says, "You shall not lie with a male as one lies with a female; it is an abomination."[2]

This did not please the pastor. He specifically faulted the elder for using God's word "abomination." In front of several other leaders, the pastor shamed this elder, saying his quotation of God's word "abomination" was "reductionistic" and his words lacked "grace."

We have arrived at a time when Christian pastors will shame members of their congregation for speaking of sin using the very words of Scripture. Do we remember Jesus' warning?

> For whoever is ashamed of Me and My words in this adulterous and sinful generation, the Son of Man will also be ashamed of him when He comes in the glory of His Father with the holy angels.[3]

The Apostle Paul lived in a culture very much like our own. Sodomy was commonplace when he wrote his letter to the Romans. Read the words of shame that the Apostle Paul uses to condemn sodomy in Romans 1 and imagine the shame church leaders and pastors would rain down on him if he wrote those words today.

Will we trust God and follow in the footsteps of the Apostle Paul and the prophets of Scripture, working to restore these biblical words and phrases to the church's witness in our own adulterous and sinful generation?

- "effeminate"
- "a man who lies with a male as those who lie with a woman"
- "detestable"

---

2. Leviticus 18:22.
3. Mark 8:38.

- "bloodguiltiness"
- "defiled"
- "abomination"
- "perversion"
- "degrading"
- "unnatural"
- "indecent"
- "depraved"[4]

Pray for God to increase your faith, then reform your public Gospel witness according to these words of Scripture inspired by the Holy Spirit in connection with homosexuality. Sure, there will be Christians who will shame you for your faithfulness. Pastors and other church leaders will condescend to inform you that the biblical language of sodomy's shame fails to demonstrate Christian compassion and love. They will explain to you that we live in a different day than New Testament times, so we must use language that communicates God's grace to our contemporaries.

But when they speak of God's "grace," they don't mean the grace of shame.

So listen to what these men say, but don't speak as they speak. Shame is the kindness of God that leads to repentance. We ourselves have seen how shame over our own sins was God's grace to us. Why would we not believe shame is God's grace to lesbians, sodomites, and the effeminate?

A South Korean newspaper recently ran an op-ed commending Confucianism and the high value it places on shame. The writer argued that recognizing one's "moral inferiority" is a good thing because it leads one to desire and strive for self-improvement. He quoted Mencius, Confucianism's second authority:

A man must not be without shame, for the shame of being without shame is shamelessness indeed.[5]

---

4. 1 Corinthians 6:9; Leviticus 20:13; Leviticus 18:22–25; Deuteronomy 22:5; Ezekiel 9:9; Romans 1:26–28. All from the NASB.

5. Kwon Bong-woon, "Teachings of Mencius," *Thoughts of the Times* (blog), *The Korea Times*, May 3, 2016, http://www.koreatimes.co.kr/www/news/opinon/2016/12/162_203943.html.

Here in the West, the context for the repudiation of sodomy's shame is shame's disappearance from public discourse. Sociologist Thomas J. Scheff notes that in the English-speaking world the use of the word "shame" has declined drastically over the past two hundred years—especially since the early sixties.[6]

Today, shame rarely means anything more significant than, "Shame on you, because I don't like you!"

The shame of the Bible is different.

In the state of perfection prior to the Fall, Adam and Eve were both naked and they were unashamed. God had made them in His image and everything He created was "good." But then, immediately following Adam's disobedience, Adam and Eve *knew* they were naked, and their shame was so great that they made themselves coverings from fig leaves and hid from their Creator.

At the beginning of his *Institutes*, John Calvin explains how shame protects us from losing all knowledge of God:

> Ever since we were stripped of the divine attire, our naked shame discloses an immense series of disgraceful properties every man, being stung by the consciousness of his own unhappiness, in this way necessarily obtains at least some knowledge of God.[7]

Reformed theologian Herman Bavinck points out that, when Adam and Eve felt shame, it was God's gift of grace:

> If immediately after the transgression a sense of guilt, shame, and fear arose in humans, then that in itself is already an operation of God's Spirit in them, indeed a revelation of His wrath but also of His grace, a revelation that is the foundation of all the religious and ethical life that still persists in humans after the Fall.[8]

Shame is a central theme of Scripture.

---

6. Thomas J Scheff, "The S-Word: Shame as a Key to Modern Societies," Global Summit On Diagnostic Alternativs, September 10, 2013, http://dxsummit.org/archives/1286.

7. *Institutes* 1.1.1.

8. *Reformed Dogmatics*, ed. John Bolt, vol. 3, *Sin and Salvation in Christ* (Grand Rapids: Baker Academic, 2006), 198.

The prophets of Israel often pointed the people to the shame of their transgressions. Thus Isaiah prophesies:

> But transgressors and sinners will be crushed together,
> And those who forsake the LORD will come to an end.
> Surely you will be ashamed of the oaks which you have desired,
> And you will be embarrassed at the gardens which you have
>   chosen.[9]

Ezekiel exhorts God's people, "Be also ashamed and bear your disgrace."[10]

Jeremiah warns Lebanon and Bashan:

> The wind will sweep away all your shepherds,
> And your lovers will go into captivity;
> Then you will surely be ashamed and humiliated
> Because of all your wickedness.[11]

In Nahum, God promises to shame Babylon:

> "Behold, I am against you," declares the LORD of hosts;
> "And I will lift up your skirts over your face,
> And show to the nations your nakedness
> And to the kingdoms your disgrace."[12]

Then, in the New Testament, the Apostle Paul condemns the Corinthian Christians for taking each other to Roman courts, writing, "I say this to your shame." Later in this letter, Paul says, "Become sober-minded as you ought, and stop sinning; for some have no knowledge of God. I speak this to your shame."[13]

Speaking to the church of Laodicea, Jesus counsels the believers

---

9. Isaiah 1:28–29.
10. Ezekiel 16:52.
11. Jeremiah 22:22.
12. Nahum 3:5.
13. 1 Corinthians 6:5; 15:34.

there, "I advise you to buy from Me gold refined by fire so that you may become rich, and white garments so that you may clothe yourself, and that the shame of your nakedness will not be revealed."[14]

Finally, Christians across the ages have trembled at our Lord's warning, "Behold, I am coming like a thief. Blessed is the one who stays awake and keeps his clothes, so that he will not walk about naked and men will not see his shame."[15]

Because shame is painful, our desire to avoid it keeps us from sin. God gave us physical pain to protect our bodies and shame to protect our souls.

A man incapable of feeling physical pain runs the risk of destroying his own body. In the same way, a shameless man risks destroying his own soul. Revealing the horror of those who have turned away from God and are headed for punishment and destruction, Scripture says they "dearly love shame" and "glory" in their shame.[16] The prophet Zephaniah declares, "The unjust know no shame."[17]

It can't be said too often that shame is God's grace.

Yes, there is false shame and it can be used as a means of oppression. In Nazi Germany, Jews were forced to wear the Yellow Star, making them feel shame for not belonging to the "Aryan race" and subjecting them to public scorn.

Thus Christians must discern the difference between true and false shame. True shame is the result of falling short of the standards set by God in His Word, whereas false shame is connected with falling short of man-made, cultural standards which have nothing to do with the standards set by God in His Word.

In Christian cultures of former times, many of their standards were aligned with God's commands, so the shame they attached to sin was a great help to souls in their pursuit of God. Now though, Westerners have thrown out God's big laws, replacing them with innumerable petty laws that flow from man's prejudices and cater to his sinful desires.[18]

---

14. Revelation 3:18.
15. Revelation 16:15.
16. Hosea 4:18; Philippians 3:19.
17. Zephaniah 3:5.
18. "When you break the big laws, you do not get liberty; you do not even get anarchy. You get the small laws." G. K. Chesterton, *Daily News*, July 29, 1905.

It's no surprise, then, that what people are shamed for today has changed, and continues to change. Take climate-change deniers, for instance. Also cigarette smokers and people who forget to fasten their seatbelts. Also people who drink soda pop, the poor souls who work with their hands for a living, and women who stay home to mother their eight (or, Heaven forbid, nine) children.

Things that were not shameful yesterday are terribly shameful today, whereas things that were shameful yesterday are required by law today. Consider sex and exposed flesh, for instance.

During the summer of 2016, news sites reported the French were outlawing burkinis. A burkini is a bathing robe that covers the arms and legs. An Australian woman invented it a few years back as a way for women to enjoy the beach without sacrificing their modesty.[19]

Muslim women of France took to wearing burkinis on the beach during the hot summer of 2016, and French officials responded by passing laws against this outbreak of modesty. French legislators banned burkinis and soon the world was treated to pictures of armed and burly French gendarmerie standing over mothers sunbathing on the beach. They measured the precise amount of flesh exposed by the matrons, and if it wasn't sufficient, the matrons received citations.

Our point here is not to bemoan the loss of past cultural standards of decency—tragic though it is.

Rather, we are working in this chapter to get Christians to wake up to what is happening around and among us. We must return to the timeless standards of honor and shame our Lord has revealed to us in His Word. But this is easier said than done. Even earnest Christians fall to the temptation of sitting in judgment on the Bible and God's words because of their desire to fit in with the cultural standards of our own times.

In past centuries, Christians recoiled in horror at even glancing references to men having sex with other men. Men who lay with males

---

19. "I wanted to do something positive—and anyone can wear this, Christian, Jewish, Hindus. It's just a garment to suit a modest person." Aheda Zanetti (Australian inventor of the burkini), "I created the burkini to give women freedom, not to take it away," *The Guardian*, August 24, 2016. Accessed October 22, 2106, https://www.theguardian.com/commentisfree/2016/aug/24/i-created-the-burkini-to-give-women-freedom-not-to-take-it-away.

were called "sodomites" because this name helped everyone feel the heat and smell the sulfur of that terrible day when God consumed the wicked men of Sodom.

Remember that it is God who hammers home the shame of men lying with males. He's the One who inspired the words "profane," "abomination," "defiled," "perversion," and "detestable." He's also the One who placed same-sex intercourse in sin lists alongside the most terribly degraded sins of incest, bestiality, and murder.[20]

Homosexualists were determined to remove sodomy's shame, and their methods weren't subtle. Since pride is the opposite of shame, they named their rebellion "gay pride," and ran their flag up the pole everywhere. They printed buttons and bumper stickers, wrote books and articles, filled the National Mall with rainbow quilts, and held ever-larger and ever-more-obscene marches down Main Streets where they paraded their shame. They have been so successful that, today, pastors and church leaders prattle on about "gay Christians," "spiritual friendship," and "homosexual orientation." Christians no longer speak of "sodomy," but merely "alternative lifestyles," and we have arrived at the point that the language of the world and the language of Christians is almost indistinguishable.

It's gotten to the point that the high point of many pastors' Gospel witness is to make a rather hesitant suggestion that "alternative lifestyles may not be God's best for human flourishing."

As poor street preachers, Jesus and His disciples were despised by the elites of their time. Thus Jesus warned his followers not to be ashamed of Him and His words. The Greek and Roman societies the Apostle Paul preached to valued high social status and intellectual sophistry. Knowing the Gospel offered neither, Paul wrote that he was "not ashamed of the Gospel" of Jesus Christ, and he called his coworker Timothy not to be ashamed of the Lord's testimony or of Paul's imprisonment.[21] Our Lord Himself was "despised and rejected by men" and suffered the shame of being crucified "outside the gate."[22]

Words matter. If we think we are wiser than God in the choice of

---

20. See Leviticus 18.
21. Romans 1:16; 2 Timothy 1:8, 16.
22. Isaiah 53:3; Hebrews 13:11–13.

words addressing same-sex sin, we prove we are fools. The reason we shy away from God's words is not because our own words are better, but because we don't want to communicate the truth which His words communicate perfectly.

One good example of the tender and sympathetic language we have adopted in the church in place of God's language is seen in the publications put out by the network of "Christians experiencing same-sex attraction" that was started a couple years ago by three Anglican pastors over in the UK. These men have recently been basking in the promotion of well-known Christian leaders across the United States.

Testifying to their Christian faith, these pastors speak of their desire to show those experiencing same-sex attraction "a plausible way of living out what Christians have consistently believed about marriage and sex."[23] They say the church of Jesus Christ has a plausibility problem among gays. She has failed men and women experiencing same-sex attraction by not allowing them to be open about their same-sex desires.

Thus they've named their organization Living Out.

The American church greeted these men ecstatically. Church leaders have been delighted to delegate to these "same-sex attracted" men the work of communicating to gays and lesbians the extremely sensitive and controversial aspects of the Christian faith's sexual ethic. The Living Out men have assured American church leaders that they know precisely which words to use to best communicate with people such as themselves.

Quite naturally, then, heterosexual church leaders who feel awkward about the absence of repentant homosexuals in their congregations and tremble at the thought of repeating the Apostle Paul's words have shown themselves desperately eager to trot these guys out on their websites and conferences as the real experts in dealing with "these people."

Dig a little deeper into LivingOut.org, though, and we begin to see the problems of subcontracting the church's Gospel witness to them. They acknowledge "homosexual behavior" is sin, yet they avoid speaking about the sin of sodomitic thoughts, feelings, and desires. Those living with sodomitic desires are to let people know about it while not acting on those desires physically.

---

23. From the LivingOut.org home page, accessed August 12, 2017.

But if sin is limited to body parts, why does the Apostle Paul warn not only "men who lie with males," but also "the effeminate," that they will not enter Heaven? If homosexual intercourse is what really matters and homosexual thinking, feeling, and desiring are allowed to fly under the radar, why did Jesus warn that "whoever looks at a woman with lust for her has already committed adultery with her in his heart"?[24]

The Bible reveals sexuality to be a much deeper part of our lives than mere physical intimacy. LivingOut.org makes some attempt to acknowledge this,[25] but where are their warnings against the sinfulness of gay identity and effeminacy?

Jesus warned the scribes and the Pharisees:

> Woe to you, scribes and Pharisees, hypocrites! For you are like whitewashed tombs which on the outside appear beautiful, but inside they are full of dead men's bones and all uncleanness.[26]

Our Lord never gave a pass to our hearts. He was relentless in His warnings against our sinful desires, lusts, and identities:

> Now you Pharisees clean the outside of the cup and of the platter; but inside of you, you are full of robbery and wickedness. You foolish ones, did not He who made the outside make the inside also?[27]

> That which proceeds out of the man, that is what defiles the man. For from within, out of the heart of men, proceed the evil thoughts, fornications, thefts, murders, adulteries, deeds of coveting and wickedness, as well as deceit, sensuality, envy, slander, pride and foolishness. All these evil things proceed from within and defile the man.[28]

Contrary to Scripture, Sean Doherty argues on LivingOut.org that warning against the sinfulness of gay thinking, feeling, and desiring

24. Matthew 5:28.
25. See Sean Doherty, "What does the Bible say about sex?" Living Out, accessed August 12, 2017, http://www.livingout.org/what-does-the-bible-say-about-sex.
26. Matthew 23:27.
27. Luke 11:39–40.
28. Mark 7:20–23.

would cause same-sex attracted individuals to experience shame, and generate the impression that "homosexuality is in some sense more problematic than being straight."[29]

"In some sense more problematic"? Seriously?

Let's substitute God's words for Mr. Doherty's words. What if Doherty were to say he prefers not to speak of the sinfulness of sodomitic thoughts, feelings, and desires because it would cause individuals tempted by sodomy to experience shame and generate the impression that sodomy is in some sense more of an abomination than being straight?

Of course, Doherty, Alberry, and the other "same-sex-attracted" men of Living Out don't want that to happen. Instead, they say they are called to "help people accept themselves as they are, just as God accepts us as we are."[30]

Really? Why does the Bible tell us how we *should* be if God accepts us as we are? Why did God give His only begotten Son, Jesus Christ, to die on the cross for our sins if God accepts us as we are? Why did God implant good shame in our hearts if He accepts us as we are? Why does Jesus call people to follow Him if God accepts us as we are? Why does the Apostle Paul call Christians to fight sin if God accepts us as we are?

Sadly, beyond the repudiation of shame implicit in their name, Living Out, these men make it explicit:

> By being open about our own experiences and journeys on this site we hope to show that there is nothing any more intrinsically shameful about same-sex attraction than about any other temptation, sexual or otherwise.[31]

So the Word of God is wrong. The apostles are wrong. The fathers of the church have all been wrong and we have this on the authority of "same-sex attracted men" like Ed Shaw who, on LivingOut.org, writes:

29. Sean Doherty, "Does Living Out support 'gay cure' or 'conversion therapy'?" Living Out, accessed August 12, 2017, http://www.livingout.org/does-living-out-support-gay-cure-or-conversion-therapy.

30. Ibid.

31. "Washed and Waiting," Living Out, accessed August 12, 2017, http://www.livingout.org/resources/washed-and-waiting.

My response to male beauty is, at one level, very natural. In desiring a beautiful man, in wanting to become one with him, I am responding to real beauty as all human beings tend to whenever, wherever, they discover it in any overwhelming form. C. S. Lewis articulates this well: "We want something else which can hardly be put into words—to be united with the beauty we see, to pass into it, to receive it into ourselves, to bathe in it, to become part of it." Is that not always the human response to incredible beauty—in a sunset, a painting, some music? You want somehow to stay and enjoy it, experience it, become part of it, forever. That's the natural effect of beauty on you. That's just how it works.

I think that will help me next time I see a beautiful man and find myself wanting to be united to him. I am, at one level, just responding to beauty as I am created to respond to it. There is little I can do to avoid this natural response. We are all wired to appreciate beauty. That's just how we work.[32]

Shaw speaks matter-of-factly about having been "wired" for the "very natural" response of wanting "to become one" with the "beautiful man" he "desires." Why should Shaw fight same-sex attraction when it is God who made him this way? "That's just the natural effect of beauty" on him. "That's just how it works." Shaw is just responding to male beauty as he is "created to respond to it."

Read through the contents of these men's writing on LivingOut.org and it's clear the horror of these quotes is no aberration. Repudiate sodomy's shame and this paean to degradation is the fruit you would expect. Ed Shaw should be horror-stricken at what he has revealed concerning his heart and its lusts, but he's lost in his shamelessness and hasn't a clue.

Note also how Living Out's repudiation of sodomy's shame goes hand-in-hand with the insinuation that sodomitic lusts are only natural for them. Then recall Calvin's warning that blaming our sin on "nature" is a devious method of making God the Author of our sin.

---

32. Ed Shaw, "How do you cope with sexual attraction as a Christian with same-sex attraction?" Living Out, accessed August 13, 2017, http://www.livingout.org/how-do-you-cope-with-sexual-attraction-as-a-christian-with-same-sex-attraction.

Yes, of course there are good things on LivingOut.org, but their good words only make their evil words more destructive to those vulnerable sheep who feed from their hands.

These men's attempt to minimize and deny sodomy's shame is no solution. When we seek to minimize or deny our guilt, we make repentance and justification impossible. It's the same with shame. When we seek to minimize or deny our shame, we are unable to cleanse our hearts and seek "the sanctification without which no one will see God."[33]

Peter was in his boat fishing and had caught nothing. Then Jesus told him to cast his nets down on the other side, and, obeying Jesus, he and his men caught so many fish that the boat was in danger of sinking under the load. Seeing this powerful manifestation of Jesus' divinity, Peter "fell down at Jesus' feet, saying, 'Go away from me Lord, for I am a sinful man!'"[34] The shame of his sinful life was more than Peter could bear, causing him to try to get away from Jesus just as Adam and Eve tried to hide from God. They all felt their shame and tried to hide.

But Jesus called Peter to be one of His disciples and promised to make him a fisher of men!

Jesus did not minimize Peter's sin and shame. Rather, from their very first meeting, Jesus provided Peter a way out of his shame. Jesus Himself gave Peter a new dignity which flowed from his faith in Jesus, the Lamb of God who takes away the sin of the world.

Today, it is the church's calling to follow our Lord's example with Peter. We are to seek ways to call people who are filled with shame to trust Jesus and repent of their sin. We are to call those covered with the shame of their sin to turn from their desire to hide and despair of themselves, trusting Jesus to wash them whiter than snow.

As He has washed each of us—praise His name!

The Gospel of Jesus Christ never minimizes shame. Rather, the Gospel removes shame through the justification of the lost, the sanctification of the believer, and the glorification of all those who belong to Christ when we pass from this world to the next. Through the work of the Holy Spirit, all who believe on the name of Jesus will "lay aside the

33. Hebrews 12:14
34. Luke 5:8.

old self, which is being corrupted in accordance with the lusts of deceit" and "put on the new self, which in the likeness of God has been created in righteousness and holiness of the truth."[35]

There's an old saying: "There are three things which the true Christian desires with respect to sin: justification, that it may not condemn; sanctification, that it may not reign; and glorification that it may not be."[36] The purposes and helpfulness of shame will not be over until we are in Heaven with our Lord, for they are given us as a grace in our fight against sin.

It is not loving to minimize or deny sodomy's shame. It is God Himself who clothed sodomy in its awful shame, and none of us have more compassion or love for those in bondage to this sin and temptation than He does. "For God so loved the world, that He gave His only begotten Son, that whoever believes in Him shall not perish, but have eternal life."

Will we turn again and trust sodomy's shame to do the work of grace in the lives of men and women who have no hope in this world or the next? Will we preach God's law to them, trusting His words "abomination," "perversion," "degraded," "unnatural," "detestable," and "depraved"; trusting His association of sodomy with the sins of bestiality, incest, and child sacrifice?

Remember our Lord's warning:

For whoever is ashamed of Me and My words in this adulterous and sinful generation, the Son of Man will also be ashamed of him when He comes in the glory of His Father with the holy angels.[37]

35. Ephesians 4:22, 24.
36. Cited as Cecil in Arthur T. Pierson, "Seed-Thoughts for Sermons and Public Discourse," *The Homiletic Review* 36 (July–December 1898), 350.
37. Mark 8:38.

For a man ought not to have his head covered, since he is the image and glory of God; but the woman is the glory of man.

1 Corinthians 11:7

CHAPTER 11

Leading Homosexuals to Repentance

THROUGHOUT THIS BOOK, WE HAVE BEEN WORKING TO demonstrate how fear of the world has corrupted our Christian witness to sexual sinners. We have called for the church to turn away from slippery words and phrases and to return to using the words of God in all their divine offense. As we've said repeatedly, speaking directly about the sinfulness of sin is true compassion, true Christian love. It is when we aren't ashamed to use Scripture's words that we find the power of the Holy Spirit at work through us for the proclamation of the Gospel and the new birth of repentant sinners.

Now we're near the end of the book, and we assume those still reading agree about the need for a forthright and biblical witness to our neighbors dying in their sins. But this forthright biblical witness is not only necessary for the church's evangelistic witness; it's also necessary for the church's work with believers—the work of Christian discipleship and sanctification.

Remember the first of the ninety-five theses Martin Luther nailed to the door of the Castle Church in Wittenberg five hundred years ago:

When our Lord and Master Jesus Christ said, "Repent," he willed the entire life of believers to be one of repentance.

Repentance isn't just something unbelievers have to do when they profess faith. Repentance is "the entire life of believers." Repentance is a gift given by the Holy Spirit at the new birth, and once begun, our work of repentance continues until death.

In the book of Hebrews, God commands Christians to pursue the "sanctification without which no one will see the Lord."[1] No man will be saved without sanctification, so something very heavy is at stake in how we speak to believers tempted by these sexual perversions.

The Apostle Paul drew a straight line between not having the blood of the Ephesians on his hands and his excruciating specificity in his preaching, teaching, and home visits:

> You yourselves know, from the first day that I set foot in Asia, how I was with you the whole time, serving the Lord with all humility and with tears and with trials which came upon me through the plots of the Jews; how I did not shrink from declaring to you anything that was profitable, and teaching you publicly and from house to house. . . .
>
> . . . Therefore, I testify to you this day that I am innocent of the blood of all men. . . . Night and day for a period of three years I did not cease to admonish each one with tears.[2]

The Apostle Paul declares he has no blood on his hands because he "did not shrink from declaring to [the Ephesians] anything that was profitable." Sadly, though, many of us today shrink from declaring God's truth to brothers and sisters in Christ who are tempted by effeminacy and sodomy:

> *Godliness is not heterosexuality. The Bible never tells us heterosexuality is good.*

---

1. Hebrews 12:14.
2. Acts 20:18–20, 26, 31.

Homosexual orientation is a sad reality. People just discover it. They come to know it at a very early age. No one freely chooses it.

We don't believe in conversion counseling. We tell pastors to stick to the simple Gospel.

I admire those gay Christian pastors who are same-sex attracted and living out on LivingOut.org.

Compare these half-truths to what the Apostle Paul said about men lying with men and women with women in a culture more sexually perverse than our own:

God gave them over to degrading passions; for their women ex-changed the natural function for that which is unnatural, and in the same way also the men abandoned the natural function of the woman and burned in their desire toward one another, men with men committing indecent acts and receiving in their own persons the due penalty of their error.[3]

Since Adam, every man has been born corrupted through and through by original sin. Man is corrupt down to his very core. Man is not a sinner because he sins, but man sins because he is a sinner.

No man can ever claim his temptations are sinless. When we are tempted, even if we don't give in to the temptation by acting on it, that temptation itself is corrupt, issuing as it does from our sinful will. Christ alone was sinless in his temptations, having no original sin.

When we weed our garden, we know that if we pull the weed off above ground, taking only what we can see and leaving the root in the soil, the weed will come back with a vengeance. So when we weed, we go for the root. The same must be our habit with sin. Whether the sin is adultery, greed, envy, or sodomy, we must not simply try to change our actions. We must cry out to God for Him to change our heart.

Jesus said:

---

3. Romans 1:26–28.

But the things that proceed out of the mouth come from the heart, and those defile the man. For out of the heart come evil thoughts, murders, adulteries, fornications, thefts, false witness, slanders. These are the things which defile the man; but to eat with unwashed hands does not defile the man.[4]

"Out of the heart." It's not enough to address our sexual sin merely by keeping our bodies from touching anyone else's body sinfully. We can't content ourselves with cleaning the outside of the cup while allowing the inside of the cup to remain filthy. Sodomitic lusts are shameful because they are contrary to nature and nature's God. Thus words and phrases such as "godliness is not heterosexuality" are destructive to everyone who hears them because these words deny that homosexuality is evil right down to the origin of this temptation in the evil heart that births it.

It's a lot easier to suppress sinful actions than sinful hearts, but God is not in the business of changing the outside of the cup. Like any good Father, His plea is, "Give me your heart, my son."[5]

We must join with our brothers and sisters in Christ, helping them to bear the grief and agony of their effeminate and sodomitic hearts. Love will lead us to work with those souls tormented by these temptations, declaring our solidarity with them as they plead with God to remove this evil that is way, way down deep inside them. And yes, this work will cause us to groan and shed tears with them as they tell us of the terrible rejection they suffered at the hands and words of their fathers. If our work of loving them is not agony, we're either not doing it from love or we're not doing it at all.

But what are we to do, instead? Will we content ourselves with giggling excitedly over gay men and lesbians who promise not to have sex with gay men and lesbians? Will we join them in denying the power of the Holy Spirit to change the sinner's heart?

This is spiritual abuse. It's pharisaical. Sure, those men in love with compromise might condemn the work of loving the effeminate and sod-

---

4. Matthew 15:18–20.
5. Proverbs 23:26.

omites as "reparative therapy," telling us we shouldn't do it, but rather content ourselves with the simple Gospel. They might assure us there's no need to weep with those who weep; that as long as they promise not to put their body parts in the wrong places, there's no need for emotional drama, let alone listening to their recounting of their childhood and sharing their agony.

But who cares what they say? Our problem with these men who heal the wounds of God's children superficially has much to do with effeminacy, little to do with sodomy, and everything to do with pastoral care—but that's for another book.

We know what it is to love our sheep, so it's our privilege to share the suffering of those with sinful temptations, working in the power of the Holy Spirit toward the end of their torment by this lust. We will work in full faith that it is the work of God to cleanse our hearts and minds—not simply our actions. We will work knowing that sinful temptations come from sinful hearts, and it's those hearts God promises to change:

> But thanks be to God that though you were slaves of sin, you became obedient from the heart to that form of teaching to which you were committed.[6]

Is it not the essence of the New Covenant that God's law will no longer be written on stone, but on our hearts?

> "But this is the covenant which I will make with the house of Israel after those days," declares the LORD, "I will put My law within them and on their heart I will write it; and I will be their God, and they shall be My people."[7]

Scripture's distinction between the outside and inside of the cup, between the sinful things that come out of the mouth and the evil in our hearts where they have their origin, is hard to hear and harder to admit and repent of. We can get our hopes up about not stealing again, but

6. Romans 6:17.
7. Jeremiah 31:33.

not wanting to steal? That seems hopeless. Like Augustine, our desire to eat other people's fruit has been there from our childhood. It's hard to remember a day when this sinful desire did not rear its ugly head and seduce us to take what wasn't ours.

How can we bear the knowledge of such sinful desires so very deep within us?

When a young father we know heard about the sinfulness of our temptations, he teared up and despairingly said that if his temptations he doesn't yield to are themselves sin, he can't go on living. It is too much—he can't bear it.

We all understand, don't we? Total depravity is a terribly heavy biblical doctrine even when it isn't misunderstood to mean we are always as bad as we could be. It's hard to look in the face of the Fall and see the corruption our father Adam brought on us all for what it really is.

French philosopher Blaise Pascal put it this way:

> For it is beyond doubt that there is nothing which more shocks our reason than to say that the sin of the first man has rendered guilty those who, being so removed from this source, seem incapable of participation in it. This transmission does not only seem to us impossible, it seems also very unjust. For what is more contrary to the rules of our miserable justice than to damn eternally an infant incapable of will, for a sin wherein he seems to have so little a share that it was committed six thousand years before he was in existence? Certainly nothing offends us more rudely than this doctrine; and yet, without this mystery, the most incomprehensible of all, we are incomprehensible to ourselves.[8]

"Incomprehensible to ourselves" because what else could explain our unlimited capacity to desire evil and give ourselves to sin? Only the Fall and corruption of original sin explain us to ourselves. Only the man who understands original sin also understands Scripture's statement that Christ reconciled us to God when we were His "enemies," and that, outside Christ, every man is a "slave" of "sin," "lawlessness," and

---

8. Blaise Pascal, *Pensées*, trans. W. F. Trotter (New York: Dover Publications, 2003), 121.

"corruption."[9] That those who don't have God as their Father have the devil as their father.[10]

The pastor or counselor working with a seeker who wants to stop hooking up with their gay or lesbian partners, and to turn to Jesus, should not apply the question of repentance to physical relations alone. Sex has meaning far deeper than how body parts are used in human intimacy. It would be conniving at the particularities of gay and lesbian sin to avoid bringing up the sexual identity God gave the seeker at the moment of his or her conception. We have to go on to call him or her to turn away from their homosexuality and embrace heterosexuality. We have to command him to turn away from his effeminacy and instead love and live his masculinity. To turn away from her bull-dykeness and instead love and live her femininity.

The seeker must repent of his effeminate sexual relations, but even more, his effeminate identity. He must repent of his homosexuality and embrace his heterosexuality. God made him a man and the beginning of his new life in Christ must be to confess his manhood.

But what if you have no theology of sexuality? What if you hate being called a "sexist" and don't want anyone to label your thinking "binary" or "dichotomous"? What if you've published and sell a version of the Bible that removes effeminacy from the sin list in 1 Corinthians 6:9–10? What if you believe manhood and womanhood have no meaning outside of copulation, baby making, and baby raising? What if you believe Adam being created first has no meaning for anyone other than Christians in the privacy of their homes and churches? What if you've published and sell a version of the Bible that removes "fit only for old women" from 1 Timothy 4:7?[11] What if you've taken the word "obey" out of the wife's vow in the marriage liturgy you use with your congregants? What if you've preached sermons reassuring your congregants that 1 Corinthians 11:6 has nothing to do with Christian worship today, and that 1 Corinthians 11:14–15 has nothing to say about the meaning of sex and the length of our hair? What if you believe Eve being deceived has no meaning for anyone other than Christians—and really,

---

9. Romans 5:10; 6:6, 19; 2 Peter 2:19.

10. John 8:44.

11. Compare NASB and ESV.

no meaning for Christians, either? What if you believe original sin is inherited from Adam and Eve, and not just Adam? What if you preach that Paul was wrong when he said man was the glory of God but woman the glory of man?

If some or all of these things are true of you, then sadly, you have no idea how to lead this seeker to confess his manhood, because manhood remains a mystery to you. This is why when someone announces that "there's no place in the Bible where heterosexuality is commanded," that "the Bible never says that heterosexuality, in general terms, is a good thing," and that "godliness is not heterosexuality," it sounds perfectly fine to you. After all, you've never thought about manhood and womanhood as the only God-given identities. To you it's merely the proper insertion of the proper body parts.

But those of us who have spent decades working with gays and lesbians know that homosexual physical relations are only the tip of the iceberg of the work of sanctification God does in their lives. Sex is so much more than copulation. Sex is who we are. Sex is who God made us and there's no part of life that escapes it. To pursue God's heterosexuality, His "male and female He created them," is to pursue holiness in matters as disparate as male clothing and female clothing, fatherhood and motherhood, male speech and female speech (and silence), male hair length and female hair length, male glory and female glory—the list is endless.

Like most things I know, I learned this through my mistakes. Years ago a young man moved from the East Coast to Bloomington in order to attend our church. He had gotten caught in homosexual bondage and wanted our pastors and elders' help toward repentance.

We have had many opera singers in our church through the years and this man sang opera, also. But he was no tenor or bass. He was a countertenor. In the olden days, young boys who showed promise as singers were castrated to keep their voices from changing. Back in the early twentieth century, Alessandro Moreschi was a member of the Sistine Chapel Choir and served as its director of soloists. Moreschi is known as "the last castrato." Fathers aren't castrating their sons so they can sing in the Vatican's choir any longer, but countertenors sound like castrati. (I know because I have seventeen tracks by Moreschi on my computer.)

Our countertenor told us he was done with homosexual relations, and I thought that was all that was needed, all we could ask. Yes, he dressed like Little Lord Fauntleroy, which is to say, effeminately. Yes, he was effeminate in his gestures and fluttered his eyes like a woman. Yes, he hung with all the gays when he was out gigging, but that was his job, wasn't it? You couldn't very well tell him to quit his job. And really, what's wrong with a man singing falsetto? Tiny Tim tiptoed through the tulips and the whole world laughed, so what's the big deal?

We understood this whole "godliness is not heterosexuality" thing quite well. We considered ourselves ever-so-progressive and enlightened, so we didn't call him to any heterosexuality other than avoiding putting his body parts where they didn't belong. What more could we ask?

He offered to sing a female aria from *Messiah* one Sunday during Advent, and I was happy for him to be making his contribution to the body of Christ. When he got up to sing, people were fishing in their purses and wallets for their offering, so at first they didn't notice that the woman's voice belonged to a man. The children noticed, though, and quickly brought their fathers and mothers up to speed. We watched as every child in the church elbowed his mother and whispered, "Mom! It sounds like a woman but it's a man!" One older elder did a double take, then reached in his pocket for his glasses and stared with incomprehension.

At the pastors' meeting that week, one of our pastors said we'd been wrong to let him sing. "He's a man and he shouldn't be leading us in worship by singing like a woman."

I didn't listen, and later in the week, as the buzz went through the church, I had several opportunities to explain to my own family and others in the church that this young man was a trained countertenor and this was how he sang. That he'd given performances around the world and we should not treat him like a pariah just because his voice wasn't stereotypically male. You all know the stuff I said because you would have agreed with me.

Sadly, though, as the years went by, this man went back into sinful sexual relations. Our elders and pastors worked with him for years, sometimes at great personal and financial expense. When he was working as an understudy at one of the opera companies on the East Coast for a few weeks and falling into sinful sexual relations, our session put one of our men on an airplane to go out and try to get him to quit his job and come home. He refused and, after several days appealing to him to flee his sin, our emissary gave up and came home. We had a subcommittee of the elders who met with this man many times to hear his confessions of sin and pray for him. Finally, after countless tearful confessions and elders' admonitions and exhortations and prayers, with great sadness our session held a trial and excommunicated the man. It was very pathetic. He was one of the very few we've excommunicated through the years who fulfilled his vow to submit to the elders by attending his trial and listening to his verdict firsthand, but there was no repentance then, nor has there been any repentance since.

After announcing his excommunication to the church, I came to see my own failures which contributed to his sin. I had not called him to be a man. I had not called him to sing like a man. I had not called him to dress and walk and relate to his women-friends as a man. I had not taught him to be a man. I had utterly failed him, and this book is a small part of my repentance.

Since then, I have understood that part of my pastoral duty is to teach men to be masculine and women to be feminine. Pastors are called by God to teach the souls under our care that from the beginning God made them male or female. God did not give them a "gender identity." He made their body male or female, and, to quote an old feminist line from the seventies, "our bodies, ourselves."

If you, dear brother or sister, are struggling with same-sex desires, don't make the terrible mistake of thinking you can limit your repentance to the physical realm. Don't think celibacy is enough. It's not. When you smile and laugh and make love and talk and walk and dress and get a haircut and garden and teach and drive and worship and study and draw and work and read the Bible and sing and pray, it all must be done to the glory of God.

So now we speak to men and women about their hair length, calling them to grow in godliness by confessing their sex through the length of their hair. It's no clear-cut thing, since masculinity and femininity of hair varies by culture, but no one ought to deny that hair length is taught by the Word of God to be a statement of faith. Of sanctification. Of godliness.

Blessed are those who have been persecuted for the sake of righteousness, for theirs is the kingdom of heaven.

Matthew 5:10

CHAPTER 12

The Way Forward

WHILE WE WERE WRITING THIS BOOK, PASTOR SAEED Abedini returned to the United States and had a joyful reunion with his loved ones. Iran freed him after almost four years of imprisonment. His crime?

An Iranian judge found him guilty of sedition. The judge closed the doors of his courtroom and had Pastor Abedini beaten in an effort to get him to admit that his real purpose for being in Iran was to overthrow the government. Pastor Abedini reports this exchange with the judge:

JUDGE. You know why you are here.

ABEDINI. Yeah, I'm here because of my Christian faith and starting the house churches. . . .

JUDGE. No, you are not here for this. You are here because you want to use Christianity to remove government.

ABEDINI. No, I don't want to do that. I just came here to start orphanage, loving people, and share the Gospel with people. And, just that.

JUDGE. No, you guys are using Christianity to remove the government. That's the reason that you are here.

ABEDINI. No, I didn't do that. I pray for you. I love you. And, I didn't come for that.

Pastor Abedini says his denial of the charge that he was trying to overthrow the government did not please the judge: "He started yelling at me, very angry."[1]

Now, a simple question. Who was right—the judge or Pastor Abedini? They both couldn't have been telling the truth, could they?

Actually, yes. Pastor Abedini was telling the truth when he denied he had come to Iran to overthrow the government, and the judge was telling the truth when he said that Pastor Abedini had come to overthrow the government. Both statements were true. Abedini was there to preach the truth of the Gospel, and the judge was right to see that truth as revolutionary.

In an Islamic nation, preaching the Gospel and building Christ's church are the most revolutionary things a man can do. True, the revolution Pastor Abedini was seeking was spiritual. He was calling men to turn from Allah to the Living God, from falsehood to truth, from slavery to freedom, from death to life.

If God blessed Pastor Abedini's work, Iran's Islamic Revolutionary courts would soon be filled with Christian converts accused of using Christianity to remove the government, and the accusations would be true. Iran is an Islamic state, after all.

But truth be told, Christian faith has become, if not revolutionary, at least unpatriotic in these United States also, and the persecution of Christians is growing in frequency and intensity. By no means do we Christians suffer here the way that Abedini did. Still, many are not content with unfriending us anymore. Now they want us removed from society and have determined to take our jobs, bankrupt our businesses, and corrupt our children.

Even in church, as we've seen in the preceding chapters, we are under pressure to stop teaching and preaching at the gaps in the wall—particularly biblical sexuality.

1. Saeed Abedini, interview by Greta Van Susteren, *FoxNews.com*, video, 0:45–1:31, January 26, 2016, http://www.foxnews.com/world/2016/01/26/christian-pastor-saeed-abedini-breaks-silence-after-being-freed-in-prisoner-swap-with-iran.html.

Political correctness prevails almost as much inside the church as it does outside; and we pastors know this, so we write, teach, and preach accordingly. It's not just the pressures pastors feel thinking of those outside the church who might judge our preaching and teaching which gets posted online. It's also that the church itself is characterized by a host of equivocations and denials of God's wonderful gift of sexuality.

Saying homosexual orientation is a real deal causes the dissonance between Sunday morning and the rest of our week to decrease. It makes us less embarrassed about inviting friends to church. We can attend family reunions without wondering which of our extended family is mad about our pastor's writing and preaching. We can take a break in the teachers' lounge and agree with everyone that it's hard to be someone with a homosexual orientation. We can agree that our school's bathroom policy should make it easier on such poor souls.

In other words, these errors this book has been working to correct don't just give bigwigs room to maneuver; they give each of us room to maneuver, also.

Today's political correctness gags God's truth everywhere. No one says it (because it's embarrassing to admit), but political correctness is almost as oppressive inside the church as it is in the public square. In our online age, political correctness stultifies Christian writing, teaching, and preaching. There is no privacy. Everything goes online and is judged by the horridly intolerant homogenization of what the most insecure and unprincipled citizens of our nation judge to be either "nice" or "mean."

This book has worked hard to demonstrate that political correctness is now gagging the Word and words of God *inside* the church.

We don't want people to attack our members outside the church because of our teaching on biblical sexuality inside the church. We don't want to alienate any of our visitors. We don't want to alienate our members who have a lesbian daughter or gay son or transsexual nephew. We don't want to alienate our elders whose wives run the show at work, then also when they get home.

But it's the rare pastor who will cop to being timid and fearful in his preaching, teaching, and pastoral care.

If you ask him, he will promise you he doesn't *ever* alter the Bible's message for fear of alienating visitors, losing members, or causing men and women of the congregation to lose their jobs. "Trust me," he says, "I would never do that. Absolutely never!"

If it's true, then he's a better man than we are. What we say in the pulpit is always written and said in the immediate awareness that Big Brother is reading and listening, and that proclaiming God's truth with authority may well cause visitors to be alienated, members to leave, or one of our members to get fired. We've only heard one man make the claim that he never dulled his preaching and teaching to make himself palatable to his people. It was the Apostle Paul, and we believe him:

> I did not shrink from declaring to you anything that was profitable, and teaching you publicly and from house to house. . . . I testify to you this day that I am innocent of the blood of all men. For I did not shrink from declaring to you the whole purpose of God. . . . Be on the alert, remembering that night and day for a period of three years I did not cease to admonish each one with tears.[2]

Why do we believe the Apostle Paul's testimony?

Because he never stopped suffering for his faithfulness to God, and much of that suffering is chronicled in his New Testament epistles, which record the constant attacks upon God's truth—not outside—but inside the church. In other words, the most important battles the Apostle Paul fought for the Gospel were against those who infiltrated the church, promoted themselves as wise men and leaders, and flattered the members of the church with false doctrine in order to gain those members as their supporters. Read the epistles: the Apostle Paul talks about this quite explicitly.

Isn't this exactly what Jesus promised His followers and their leaders?

> Blessed are those who have been persecuted for the sake of
> righteousness, for theirs is the kingdom of heaven.

> Blessed are you when people insult you and persecute you, and
> falsely say all kinds of evil against you because of Me. Rejoice and

---

2. Acts 20:20, 26–27, 31.

be glad, for your reward in heaven is great; for in the same way they persecuted the prophets who were before you.[3]

Coming under pressure from within and without the church for your Christian witness to God's Creation Order of man and woman is suffering persecution "for the sake of righteousness." So "rejoice and be glad" because you are living in solidarity with Isaiah, Jeremiah, Hosea, Micah, Jonah, John the Baptist, our Lord Jesus, and the Apostle Paul.

If you have not felt such pressure for your Christian witness to God's Creation Order of man and woman, what world are you living in? Maybe you've been up in the space station for three hundred days? Maybe you're a Trappist monk who's taken a vow of silence? If that is who you are and how you care for the souls purchased by our Savior's blood, have you forgotten your Savior's words?

> Remember the word that I said to you, "A slave is not greater than his master." If they persecuted Me, they will also persecute you; if they kept My word, they will keep yours also. But all these things they will do to you for My name's sake, because they do not know the One who sent Me.[4]

Did you ever notice how the Apostle Paul ends his battle with the Judaizers recorded in his letter to the Galatians? Two statements in Galatians are particularly precious to us as pastors seeking to grow in boldness and faithfulness to God as we shepherd the souls bought with the blood of His precious Son.

The first is this plaintive lament that comes out of Paul unbidden in the heat of battle: "So have I become your enemy by telling you the truth?"[5]

The second is this demand, when, very weary, he draws the battle to an end: "From now on let no one cause trouble for me, for I bear on my body the brand-marks of Jesus."[6]

Sometimes we wonder if the Apostle Paul sat through elders' meet-

3. Matthew 5:10–12.
4. John 15:20–21.
5. Galatians 4:16.
6. Galatians 6:17.

ings where he was on the chopping block because he'd caused the riot
led by Demetrius which resulted in the mob of Ephesians being "filled
with rage" and for two hours crying out, "Great is Artemis of the Ephesians! Great is Artemis of the Ephesians!"[7]

Is there ever a time when persecution couldn't have been avoided by
a little postponement, a little compromise, a little more tact? Did Jesus
really have to die? Do we really have to take up our cross and follow
Him? Is it really necessary for us to be persecuted like our Master was?
Must we really be hated? Must we really witness to our faith publicly?
What was John the Baptist thinking when he told Herod he ought not
have his brother's wife? Didn't he realize he would lose his head? Was
there no one who cared enough to warn him?

Then there's the Apostle Paul—why all the danger and suffering?

Again, please think about all this and ask the Lord for truth in your
inward parts.

There is no such thing as perfection in our witness to the Gospel
today. Each of us has our own sins and temptations and we will see
those sins and temptations in everything we do and say, including our
Gospel witness. We all know the routine: Satan tempts us to be silent
until we're perfect, and then he makes sure we're never perfect so we're
always silent. Perfectionism is the perfect gag for Christians.

But if we wait until we're perfect to witness to the world of sin and
righteousness and judgment, we'll never do it at all. Never.

Is this how we want to live—ashamed of Jesus and His words?
Wouldn't we rather tell Herod he ought not have his brother's wife and
lose our head for it? I mean, really? Imagine the joy when John the Baptist and the Apostle Paul died and stood before our Lord to hear from
His lips this most precious of all eulogies:

Well done, good and faithful slave. You were faithful with a few
things, I will put you in charge of many things; enter into the joy
of your master.

Matthew 25:23

---

7. See Acts 19:23–41.

With notes from Tim . . .

By the Author

Bayly, Tim. *Daddy Tried: Overcoming the Failures of Fatherhood.*
Bloomington, IN: Warhorn Media, 2016.
Those wanting to grow in their repentance from effeminacy
would do well to read this book by one repentant effeminate.
Single men should read it too because every man—married or
single, childless or with a quiver full—has been called to fatherhood from the moment of his conception.

Essential Reading

Butterfield, Rosaria. *The Secret Thoughts of an Unlikely Convert: An
English Professor's Journey into Christian Faith.* Pittsburgh, PA:
Crown & Covenant Publications, 2012.
The personal account of a deconstructionist English professor
who came to Christian faith, and, leaving her lesbian partner,
learned to love and live the sex God made her.

Cantarella, Eva. *Bisexuality in the Ancient World.* Translated by Cor-
mac Ó Cuilleanáin. New Haven, CT: Yale University Press,
2002.
No book has been more helpful to my understanding of the
manipulations and deceptions of the homosexuals today. An
Italian classicist, Cantarella opens up the bisexuality of Ancient

Greece and Rome in such a way as to give us a place to stand in opposing all the purveyors of that non-thing hawked as "gender identity" or "homosexual orientation." Cantarella argues there was no such thing in the ancient world.

Chesterton, G. K. *What's Wrong with the World.* https://www.ccel .org/ccel/chesterton/whatwrong.html.
No one is more helpful in learning how to think about male and female. No one.

———. *The Thing.* http://www.gkc.org.uk/gkc/books/The_Thing .txt.
This contains the single essay I've read aloud to more people than any other. Titled "The Drift from Domesticity," it begins, "In the matter of reforming things, as distinct from deforming them . . ." I despair to think of the stupidity that would cloud my preaching, teaching, and writing if I'd never read Chesterton. Read these essays and consider that he wrote them a century ago. To call him prescient doesn't begin to express it.

Clark, Stephen B. *Man and Woman in Christ: An Examination of the Roles of Men and Women in Light of Scripture and the Social Sciences.* Servant Books, 1980.
Clark's work remains the best treatment of biblical sexuality. The work is very long with lots of footnotes and endnotes, but it is a must-read. Clark is to feminism what Gagnon is to homosexuality.

Elliot, Elisabeth. *Let Me Be a Woman.* Carol Stream, IL: Tyndale House, 1976.
Like Rosaria Butterfield today, the late Elisabeth Elliot was the woman men pushed forward to do the dirty work of fighting the sexual anarchists infiltrating the church. Across the thirty-some years of our work in the pastorate, my wife Mary Lee and I have been greatly strengthened by Elliot's witness and writing.

Gagnon, Robert A. J. *The Bible and Homosexual Practice: Texts and Hermeneutics.* Nashville: Abingdon Press, 2001.

Gagnon is something like our Athanasius against the homosexualist heretics. Gagnon has long been hard at work exposing the lies religious leaders employ to normalize the homosexual perversion within the church. This work is the best defense of the historic church's interpretation of Scripture's condemnations of sodomy and lesbianism. Gagnon is to homosexuality what Clark is to feminism.

Mayer, Lawrence S., and Paul R. McHugh. "Sexuality and Gender: Findings from the Biological, Psychological, and Social Sciences." *The New Atlantis,* no. 50 (Fall 2016). http://www.thenewatlantis .com/docLib/20160819_TNA50ExecutiveSummary.pdf.

A survey of the literature, with or without an education you can understand the things in this report that are important for our work with those suffering LGBTQ temptations. Mayer is a scholar in residence and McHugh a professor of psychiatry and behavioral sciences at Johns Hopkins University School of Medicine. McHugh was psychiatrist-in-chief at Johns Hopkins Hospital for twenty-five years.

Morrison, Steve. *Born This Way: Making sense of science, the Bible and same-sex attraction.* Matthias Media, 2015.

A new book that is short, simple, and thoroughly biblical. The book you give young Christians wanting (or not wanting) to learn how to stand on the issue their Christian witness will suffer more shaming for than any other.

Ozment, Steven. *When Fathers Ruled: Family Life in Reformation Europe.* Cambridge, MA: Harvard University Press, 1983.

This book by a renowned Reformation scholar reformed my understanding of the Reformation by opening up the radical recovery of fatherhood at its core. Calvin scholar Robert Kingdon: "This is a splendid book" containing "fascinating fresh evidence."

Schaumburg, Harry. *Undefiled: Redemption from Sexual Sin, Restoration for Broken Relationships.* Chicago: Moody Publishers, 2009.

Schaumburg is mandatory reading for those tormented by sinful lusts who are seeking repentance. Also, I recommend Schaumburg's intensive counseling program for couples. See StoneGateResources.org.

Shilts, Randy. *And the Band Played On: Politics, People, and the AIDS Epidemic.* New York: St. Martin's Press, 1988.

Tragic account of the AIDS epidemic by a journalist at the *San Francisco Chronicle* who observed the epidemic firsthand, later succumbing to AIDS himself. This work is to the homosexualist movement of the eighties what Eldrige Cleaver's *Soul on Ice* and *The Autobiography of Malcolm X* were to the civil rights movement of the sixties.

Watson, Thomas. *The Christian Soldier,* or *Heaven Taken by Storm.* Accessed August 14, 2017. http://www.fivesolas.com/watson/soldie _i.htm.

Watson is always helpful in a manly way. He's a Puritan so his writing is direct and doesn't flatter. This work is an exposition of Jesus' commendation of the violent, manly pursuit of the kingdom of God.

————. *The Doctrine of Repentance.* Edinburgh: Banner of Truth Trust, 1988.

Once we get it, that our sex is a station in life given us by God at the moment of conception, and that it is our duty and privilege to learn to live and love it, we'll spend the rest of our lives repenting of all the ways we rebel against our station, whether we are male or female. All of us are rebels against our sex, albeit in various ways at various times and with different degrees of intensity. Watson's very short treatment of the grace of repentance is helpful to those committed to sanctification in our sexuality.

Wilson, Doug. *Future Men.* Moscow, ID: Canon Press, 2012.

A book on raising sons, by a former submariner who has shown me how to repent of my indecision and fear in my work as a pastor.

Also Recommended

Bellos, David. *Is That a Fish in Your Ear?: Translation and the Meaning of Everything.* New York: Farrar, Straus and Giroux, 2011.

For those interested in pursuing the question why modern Bible translators can't seem to help themselves in adding and deleting words from Scripture. Bellos is a Princeton professor who has won awards for his translations. Here, he explains, as only a pagan can and would, why Wycliffe Bible Translators and other Bible translators refuse to give Scripture to us straight.

Blamires, Harry. *The Christian Mind.* London: SPCK, 1968.

In our evil age of sexual anarchy, thinking biblically is the very beginning of Christian witness. This book is entertaining, if you can believe it, providing all of us lazy-brain Christians a good stiff kick in the posterior sufficient to bust us loose from the rhetorical ploys and lies permeating the church. Blamires punches in the same weight class as Chesterton, Lewis, and Sayers.

Bloesch, Donald G. *The Battle for the Trinity: The Debate over Inclusive God-Language.* Eugene, OR: Wipf and Stock, 2001.

This short and accessible work by a neo-orthodox theologian demonstrates that today's sexual anarchy is an attack upon the everlasting Fatherhood of God. Bloesch warns those who will not address God as "Father" that they have denied the Christian faith.

Brown, Peter. *The Body and Society: Men, Women and Sexual Renunciation in Early Christianity.* New York: Columbia University Press, 1988.

A classic by a patristics scholar without equal.

Crompton, Louis. *Homosexuality and Civilization*. Cambridge, MA: Harvard University Press, 2003.

It's always good to know your enemies and this work is as good as all the other thousands of books written by men and women with the terminal degree who glory in their shame. The *Los Angeles Times* commends it: "Brilliantly researched. . . . Crompton, drawing on his immense erudition, contrasts Christianity and its barbaric cruelty toward same-sex love with more benign traditions in Moorish Spain . . ." Right.

Douglas, Ann. *The Feminization of American Culture*. New York: Farrar, Straus and Giroux, 1998.

A classic.

Foucault, Michel. *The Care of the Self*. Vol. 3 of *The History of Sexuality*. New York: Vintage Books, 1988.

A classic.

Gilder, George. *Men and Marriage* (formerly titled *Sexual Suicide*). Gretna, LA: Pelican Publishing, 1992.

An unbeliever opens up the civilizing (Christians would say "sanctifying") influence marriage provides for men. Also the horror that results when men stop marrying.

Grossman, Miriam. *Unprotected: A Campus Psychiatrist Reveals How Political Correctness in Her Profession Endangers Every Student*. New York: Sentinel, 2007.

Worth reading.

Harper, Kyle. *From Shame to Sin: The Christian Transformation of Sexual Morality in Late Antiquity*. Cambridge, MA: Harvard University Press, 2013.

A new work worth reading. It's a shame to say Harper seems unaware of the divine purpose and Christian meaning and context of shame and sin.

Hubbard, Thomas K., ed. *Homosexuality in Greece and Rome: A Sourcebook of Basic Documents.* Berkeley: University of California Press, 2003.
Primary sources on same-sex lust in the ancient world. Not for the timid.

Hutt, Corinne. *Males and Females.* London: Penguin, 1972.
Old enough to be objective. Still, way back in 1972 the author put this on the cover: "I make no apology for stating the case for the biological bases of psychological sex differences." *Times Literary Supplement*: "An excellent introduction to one of the most interesting and important areas of study of mankind."

John Paul II. *Familiaris Consortio (On the Family).* http://w2.vatican .va/content/john-paul-ii/en/apost_exhortations/documents/hf_ jp-ii_exh_19811122_familiaris-consortio.html
If you haven't read it, do so. In moral theology, Roman Catholics have been light years ahead of Protestants.

Kevan, Ernest F. *The Grace of Law: A Study of Puritan Theology.* Grand Rapids: Soli Deo Gloria Publications, 2003.
Kevan's title is the inspiration for "the grace of shame." The grace of God's law is a foreign concept to us and serves as a good introduction to the grace of shame.

Knox, John. *The First Blast of the Trumpet Against the Monstrous Regiment of Women.* http://www.gutenberg.org/ebooks/9660.
Like Edwards's "Sinners in the Hands of an Angry God," this work by the Protestant reformer is much-maligned and rarely read. John Calvin disapproved of Knox's purpose and timing when he wrote and released this book anonymously, but Calvin agreed with the substance of Knox's work.

Manetsch, Scott M. *Calvin's Company of Pastors: Pastoral Care and the Emerging Reformed Church, 1536–1609.* Oxford: Oxford University Press, 2013.

This is a recommendation for pastors, elders, deacons, and Titus 2 women. If we are going to be helpful to those repenting of sexual rebellion, we simply must recover the work of pastoral care for the Protestant church. Manetsch does a superb job documenting how foundational pastoral care was to Calvin and the Genevan church in the time of the Reformation.

Mead, Margaret. *Male and Female: A Study of the Sexes in a Changing World*. New York: William Morrow & Co., 1949.
A classic by the *grande dame* of anthropologists.

Merkle, Rebekah. *Eve in Exile and the Restoration of Femininity*. Moscow, ID: Canon Press, 2016.
Doug Wilson's daughter. The likeness is evident in the helpfulness of Merkle's teaching.

Mouser, Bill, and Barbara Mouser. *Five Aspects of Man* and *Five Aspects of Woman*. Waxahachie, TX: International Council for Gender Studies.
Bill and Barbara are dear friends who have developed and teach this church curriculum on sexuality. The Mousers give simple and direct explanations of the meaning and purpose of sexuality across God's creation.

Neuer, Werner. *Man and Woman in Christian Perspective*. Translated by Gordon J. Wenham. Wheaton, IL: Crossway, 1991.
More nuanced and philosophical than Clark, but helpful. German systematic theologian.

Newell, Waller R., ed. *What Is A Man?: 3000 Years of Wisdom on the Art of Manly Virtue*. New York: ReganBooks, 2001.
Compilation of historical sources on manhood by Aristotle, Augustine, Jane Austen, Kurt Cobain, Hemingway, Twain, Frederick Douglass, et al.

Quay, Paul M. *The Christian Meaning of Human Sexuality*. San Francisco: Ignatius Press, 1985.
Fr. Paul Quay was a dear friend and I commend his short work providing an extended Trinitarian meditation on sexuality.

Rhoads, Steven E. *Taking Sex Differences Seriously*. San Francisco: Encounter Books, 2004.
Worth reading.

Rosin, Hanna. *The End of Men: And the Rise of Women*. New York: Riverhead Books, 2012.
Best-seller. The *Washington* Post says, "Anchored by data and aromatized by anecdotes, [Rosin] concludes that women are gaining the upper hand."

Sayers, Dorothy. *Unpopular Opinions*. New York: Harcourt, Grace and Company, 1947.
Her little essay "Are Women Human?" is necessary reading for every Christian woman and every man who loves any Christian woman.

Sexton, Patricia Cayo. *The Feminized Male*. New York: Random House, 1969.
Schools are designed for girls, not boys.

Smith, Helen. *Men on Strike: Why Men are Boycotting Marriage, Fatherhood, and the American Dream—and Why It Matters*. New York: Encounter Books, 2013.
Worth reading.

Welch, Edward T. *Addictions: A Banquet in the Grave: Finding Hope in the Power of the Gospel*. Phillipsburg, NJ: P&R Publishing, 2001.
As helpful as Schaumburg.

Witte, John, Jr., and Robert Kingdon. *Sex, Marriage, and Family in Calvin's Geneva*. Vol. 1, *Courtship, Engagement, and Marriage*. Grand Rapids: Wm. B. Eerdmans Publishing Co., 2005.

I had the privilege of studying under Kingdon while getting my undergraduate degree in history at University of Wisconsin–Madison. As a Calvin scholar, Kingdon had few (if any) equals. Now, thanks to his work, we have many new English sources on the pastoral work of Calvin and his company of pastors which those desiring to grow in our leadership and service to those suffering under their own and others' sexual sin would do well to read.

THE CONFESSIONS *OF AMERICAN CHRISTIANS RECOVERING FROM* AMERICAN CHRISTIANITY

WARHORN MEDIA PODCAST

Season 1 of *The World We Made* features interviews with author Tim Bayly discussing homosexuality.

Find this and more great content at
WarhornMedia.com

CPSIA information can be obtained
at www.ICGtesting.com
Printed in the USA
FFOW02n2344290817